CRACKING GOOD BOOKS

Teaching literature at Key Stage 2

Judith Graham

NATE

Cracking Good Books is published by the National Association for the Teaching of English (NATE), the UK subject teacher association for all aspects of the teaching of English from pre-school to university.

NATE
50 Broadfield Road
Sheffield S8 0XJ

Tel: 0 114 255 5419
Fax: 0 114 255 5296
E-mail: nate.hq@campus.bt.com

British Library Cataloguing in Publication Data. A catalogue record for this book is available from the British Library.

ISBN 0 901291 51 X

© Judith Graham 1997
First published 1997; fourth impression 1998

This work is copyright but copies may be made of pages 26–31 and the pupil pages without fee or prior permission provided that these copies are used solely within the institution for which it is purchased. For copying in other circumstances (i.e. by an external resource centre) prior written permission must be obtained from the Publisher and a fee may be payable.

Design and illustration by Ken Brooks

Edited by Dodi Beardshaw

Printed in the United Kingdom by
York Publishing Services Ltd, 64 Hallfield Road, Layerthorpe, York YO3 7XQ

Contents

Introduction		5
Titles and levels of 'difficulty'		7
Authors and illustrators		9
Teacher pages		10
Pupil pages		22
Pupil response sheets		24
Conclusion		25
Sheets 1–6		26

Suitable for Year 3

1. *Julian, Dream Doctor* by Ann Cameron — 32
   Illustrated by Ann Strugnell

2. *Thomas and the Tinners* by Jill Paton Walsh — 34
   Illustrated by Alan Marks

3. *Grace & Family* by Mary Hoffman — 36
   Illustrated by Caroline Binch

4. *The Shape-Changer* by Julian Atterton — 38
   Illustrated by Nigel Murray

5. *Storm* by Kevin Crossley-Holland — 40
   Illustrated by Alan Marks

Suitable for Year 4

6. *Harry, the Poisonous Centipede* by Lynne Reid Banks — 42
   Illustrated by Tony Ross

7. *'The chicken gave it to me'* by Anne Fine — 44
   Illustrated by Philippe Dupasquier

8. *Harriet's Hare* by Dick King-Smith — 46
   Illustrated by Valerie Littlewood

9. *The Little Riders* by Margaretha Shemin — 48
   Illustrated by Peter Spier

10. *Sir Gawain and the Green Knight* retold by Selina Hastings — 50
    Illustrated by Juan Wijngaard

11. *Celebration Song* by James Berry — 52
    Illustrated by Louise Brierley

12. *The Battle of Bubble and Squeak* by Philippa Pearce — 54
    Illustrated by Alan Baker

Suitable for Year 5

13. *The Winter Sleepwalker* by Joan Aiken — 56
    Illustrated by Quentin Blake

14. *The Highwayman* by Alfred Noyes — 58
    Illustrated by Charles Keeping

15. *Princess Jazz and the Angels* by Rachel Anderson — 60

16. *The Pied Piper of Hamelin* by Robert Browning — 62
    Illustrated by André Amstutz

	17	*The Wreck of the Zanzibar* by Michael Morpurgo *Illustrated by Christian Birmingham*	64
	18	*Five Children and It* by E. Nesbit *Illustrated by H. R. Millar*	66
Suitable for Year 6	19	*The Stinky Cheese Man and Other Fairly Stupid Tales* by Jon Scieszka *Illustrated by Lane Smith*	68
	20	*The Firework-Maker's Daughter* by Philip Pullman *Illustrated by Nick Harris*	70
	21	*Harvey Angell* by Diana Hendry	72
	22	*Children of Winter* by Berlie Doherty *Illustrated by Ian Newsham*	74
	23	*The Great Elephant Chase* by Gillian Cross	76
	24	*The Finding* by Nina Bawden	78

Introduction

The title *Cracking Good Books* plays pleasingly with words but in the process begs a few questions. My choice of what are 'cracking good books' may not be yours and it may not be the choice of your pupils. Twenty-four books are rather few to present in the hope that all will find something to enjoy. Do twenty-four universally popular books for children exist? Probably not, but if they do then you certainly know them all already. Bestseller charts for children of this age usually include a Roald Dahl title or two, perhaps Ted Hughes' *The Iron Man* and certainly a handful of 'Goosebumps' titles. If these are your favourites too you will not need an introduction to them here. I have deliberately chosen some lesser known titles in this collection.

Primarily, however, I have chosen books that I have enjoyed reading and, more importantly, re-reading and which, when it came to developing ideas for pupil activities, revealed strengths across the board. The books had good story structure: their plots were strong and tight and yet not wholly predictable. They had people in them that I cared to spend time with and whom I went on thinking about. They created fictitious landscapes in my head against which the characters moved and I believed in their various 'secondary worlds'. I found much to reflect on in their messages to their child readers and I found myself willing to attend to and take pleasure from their language. My final choice, my two dozen from the hundred plus that I initially considered, meet these criteria. They, the 'fittest' ones, survived.

Let us return to the other meaning of 'cracking'. To crack something means, colloquially at least, to understand it and I have presumed to share my interpretations, my emphases, my analyses of these books. Yet, once again, my understanding, my 'reading', of the children's books presented here may not be yours and may not be your pupils'. 'Cracking' of a book can only ever be personal. In addition, to 'crack' something implies understanding it for ever but the interpretation of art forms, including children's books, changes and develops throughout our lives. How I have cracked these twenty-four books today may not be how I would crack them tomorrow.

What I could now conclude is that there is no place for this book and that all such books run risks of narrowing the range of interpretations and responses. I think I can justify my efforts on three counts. Firstly, I have tried, in the teacher page (the left-hand page) for each book, to provide a straightforward and useful breakdown of the book from which teachers can readily develop ideas and activities of their own. Secondly, in the pupil page (the right-hand page), I have tried to keep the activities to tasks that reflect the individual book's strengths. Thirdly, I have tried to make the pupil tasks enjoyably purposeful and creative in themselves. I shall develop these points in the relevant sections that follow.

Part of me now wants to be less cautious however and state that there *is* a need for a book such as this. In a world without pressure, without tests and imposed requirements, children's reading could be centre-stage in the classroom, with whole weeks given over to the reading and discussion of literature. Story time and private reading time could happen several times a day. Teachers would have time to read widely, talk at length with their classes about books and develop exciting projects. Life is not like that anymore and literature teaching particularly has suffered in the squeeze of the primary school curriculum. HMI recognised this (1990):

In Key Stage 2, reading received less systematic attention as the children grew older and other demands arose from the widening curriculum. By Year 6, three-quarters of the children assessed were reading widely on their own but the majority was not being challenged to develop advanced reading skills.

Teachers also feel that with less time they must work ever more efficiently. Every book chosen must be significant; every activity undertaken must be beneficial. Teachers are looking, as they always have, for stimulating material that will help them to teach well.

This book is not intended to be a short-cut nor a manual for the teaching of literature for teachers. It is hoped that it could be a resource and an aide-mémoire. It may even prove to be a basis for developing literature work generally with a different set of titles. At the very least it may whet appetites about new or unknown children's books, give ways of thinking about their features and provide ideas for their teaching.

In the sections that follow, the rationale behind the different headings of the teacher and pupil pages is explained. Further points and suggestions are made and a comprehensive overview of the books is given so that teachers can select for specific reasons and in order to ensure a range and a balance.

I would like to acknowledge the support and interest of teachers, students at Roehampton Institute, family, children, colleagues and friends, particularly that of my colleague at Roehampton Institute, Fiona M. Collins.

Titles and levels of 'difficulty'

Although the twenty-four titles are arranged in an order, it is not possible to say with any certainty that one title is more suitable for a particular age group than another. Children continually surprise us in their choice of, and their stamina with, books and, of course, like adults they move around a great deal between 'easier' and more 'difficult' books. Broadly, in grouping the titles under Year groups, I have tried to assess and balance the following:

- challenges in the language and concepts
- emotional challenge
- complexity of the plot
- ages of the characters
- presence or otherwise of illustrations
- cover appeal
- layout of the page
- type size
- length of chapters
- length of the book
- 'implied reader' of the book.

These are ways in which the author and publisher reach out, or fail to reach out, to readers. A few examples will help here.

The language in *Grace & Family* may be simple, and the illustrations may help to bring the locations alive, but the concept in the book (trying to fuse the conventional view of a family with the reality) is less straightforward and may challenge some Year 3s. Conversely, the rich, figurative language of *The Winter Sleepwalker* may appear to make this title beyond the grasp of younger or less experienced readers. Yet, because it is a book of short stories, because it echoes the patterns of many traditional tales and because its ideas and language are so appealing, it may be less challenging than first appears. There are six titles in this collection that are picture books but they are certainly not the 'easiest' titles. In the case of *The Highwayman*, the portrayed violence may rule it out of the primary school totally for some teachers. *The Pied Piper of Hamelin* and *Sir Gawain and the Green Knight* are both in picture book format, but whilst pictures certainly add to their accessibility and help pupils with the archaisms to some extent, they do not thereby become books for the youngest children. Indeed I have included *Sir Gawain and the Green Knight* with some trepidation because, in many people's view, it is a most erotic tale. It is also one of the most wonderful to have in any literary store. *Harriet's Hare*, a title that young Dick King-Smith fans will seize enthusiastically, is also included somewhat nervously, as its robust attitude to the importance of mating may not be deemed suitable to all. And one could go on. All teachers know of children who seem to conquer all sorts of textual difficulties to get at the books they really want to read.

Perhaps matching the book to the age of the reader can be achieved by checking on the age of its main character. Julian in *Julian, Dream Doctor* is eight; Annie in *Storm* is nine. These titles are certainly appreciated by children of the same age. But Thomas in *Thomas and the Tinners* and the young people in *The Shape-Changer* are of an age to work and to fall in love and yet the evidence is that eight and nine year olds are the implied readers of these books. Children certainly like reading about children (and adults) older than themselves. They seem to be trying these older people's lives on for size. But many also read quite happily about children who are the age that they were themselves not so long ago. And the age of many characters, particularly that of animal characters, is often not specified. So perhaps the protagonist's ages are not such a useful guide.

In the end, the emotional truth of the book may be what sells it to any particular age. Julian in *Julian, Dream Doctor* longs to give his father the best ever present and finds he has helped his dad to overcome a fear. This makes it a story to resonate with seven and eight year olds; the self-sacrifice of Bess in *The Highwayman* is not so likely to touch them. The amazing, defiant determination of Lila in *The Firework-Maker's Daughter* is surely of more interest to ten and eleven year olds than it is to seven year olds for whom the naughtiness of Harry and his friend in *Harry, the Poisonous Centipede* maps more accurately on to life as they know it.

The order in which the books appear here is influenced by such interconnecting aspects of each book. As has always been the case, there is no substitute for knowing your children and the books well. Teachers' own judgements of when to introduce the books to their pupils are always the best.

Authors and illustrators

Almost all authors and illustrators of the presented books are still living. The exceptions are the original, unknown teller of *Sir Gawain and the Green Knight*, the poets Robert Browning and Alfred Noyes, the writer E. Nesbit and the illustrator Charles Keeping.

Amongst the authors, only Margaretha Shemin is relatively unknown. Her book, *The Little Riders*, is the accessible telling of a suspenseful, war-time story, with non-stereotypical characters and a believable child heroine; it was such a find that I felt it deserved a place. Some authors, such as Dick King-Smith, are so well known that they need no promotion but it was exciting to find that the scrutiny to which I subjected *Harriet's Hare* exposed an even more impressive writer than I had originally believed.

Amongst the picture book illustrators, Charles Keeping is perhaps the most eminent. Caroline Binch, the illustrator of *Grace & Family*, is becoming well known as an illustrator of black characters; Louise Brierley's strong sculptural shapes or, conversely, her stick figures suit the mythic material she often illustrates. Juan Wijngaard captures period well in his meticulous work. André Amstutz's cheerful work is familiar to readers of Allan Ahlberg's *Funnybones* books and the American Lane Smith is recognisable from his work in *The True Story of the Three Little Pigs*. Amongst the line and colour illustrators of the fiction, familiar names such as Tony Ross, Alan Marks, Philippe Dupasquier, Peter Spier and Quentin Blake can be found in supporting roles and we cannot underestimate the role such illustration plays in helping to lift the words off the page for the reader. Nick Harris illustrates exuberantly in *The Firework-Maker's Daughter*; his contribution to that book's popularity needs recognition.

Most of the authors are British. We are fortunate to have great children's books in this country but it is regrettable that more titles from abroad are not published here. Margaretha Shemin's *The Little Riders* comes originally from Holland, *Julian, Dream Doctor* comes from the USA as does *The Stinky Cheese Man and Other Fairly Stupid Stories* but otherwise this list looks fairly parochial. To compensate, several of the books chosen at least throw their net beyond our shores as we shall see when we discuss stories and settings.

Of the 24 authors, 9 are male and 15 are female. Male illustrators predominate, with 16 male and 4 female. Four books are unillustrated.

Teacher pages

Publication details In all cases, the illustrator's name is given as well as the author's. It is time that the role of the illustrator in children's reading development is better acknowledged. Children have always taken notice of illustrations; they use them to lift the words off the page into images, focal points and ideas in their head. We must not inadvertently train them to disregard them.

This information is followed by the date and publisher of the first (hardback) publication, and the date and publisher of the subsequent paperback edition. The ISBN number given is always of the paperback and it is the paperback version that I have used. Paperbacks usually cost less than half the price of the hardback and many readers prefer them. In any case, budgets dictate paperbacks in most schools, especially for group sets. Nevertheless, individual library copies of novels and picture books are still commonly purchased in hardback and, if only a hardback is available, teachers should find few disadvantages and some advantages. The hardbacks of *The Wreck of the Zanzibar* and *The Winter Sleepwalker* are particularly pleasing in production terms compared with their paperbacks. In the case of *Sir Gawain and the Green Knight*, however, it is preferable to have the paperback which has, unusually, additional illustrations. In the ten years between the hardback and the paperback versions, Juan Wijngaard had won the Kate Greenaway Award for a second book, *Sir Gawain and the Loathly Lady*, and he wanted to bring the first title up to those high standards. In addition, the publisher, Walker Books, had developed a clearer vision of how they wanted their picture books to look and they improved the design of the book.

Genre Genre is a term which was not much in use in any discussion of children's literature until a few years ago. I use it here because no other term quite covers both the sense of different categories of book and the different types of book within those categories.

The National Curriculum uses the word *categories*, under which at Key Stage 2 it puts a range of modern fiction by significant children's authors; some long-established children's fiction; a range of good quality modern poetry; some classic poetry; texts drawn from a variety of cultures and traditions; myths, legends and traditional stories. The texts presented in this book fit well into one or more of these categories. By Key Stages 3 and 4, the National Curriculum is using the term different *genres* to mean plays, novels, short stories and poetry.

Different *types* of books were traditionally divided into sections in libraries and elsewhere, such as: adventure, animal, fantasy, realism, mystery, ghost, magic, long ago, other lands, humour, family, school, love, etc. These divisions are useful, though of course many books have characteristics of more than one type. In the twenty-four books here, there are not many examples of the old adventure story; adventures usually come along with legend or fantasy or history.

For the genre theorists whose work on the identification of the linguistic features and characteristics of different text types – broadly, how narrative and non-narrative texts are organised – the relaxed use here of the word *genre* is probably unacceptable but it enables me to give, under its heading, as succinct a description of the sort of book under consideration as possible.

Narrative voice and devices

Impersonal narrator: Probably the majority of narratives are told by an impersonal narrator, who reports on events without an evaluative or personal comment. Typically, the impersonal narrator uses characters' names and the corresponding pronouns 'they', 'he' and 'she'. The narrative is then called a third person narrative. Neither 'I' (first person) nor 'you' (second person) is used. The narrator does not make appeals to us as readers. Classic impersonal, third person narratives in this collection are: *Thomas and the Tinners*, *Grace & Family*, *Storm*, *The Little Riders*, *Sir Gawain and the Green Knight* and *The Highwayman*.

Within a third person narration, there is often a character whom the narrator privileges. In *The Shape-Changer* for instance we are in no doubt that Kari is the character whom the narrator has his eye on at all times yet we do not hear his inner thoughts, only see his actions and hear his speech. In texts such as this, one of the pupil activities is designed to bring out the inner thoughts of the character. In other texts, the impersonal narrator does give us access to a character's thought processes. In *Princess Jazz and the Angels* we are allowed glimpses into Jazz's mind: 'Another long hour passed and grew into another long day. Jazz grew restless. Surely Bridie must come to find her soon?' In texts such as this, there is a pupil activity that enables the reader to reflect that other characters in the book must have viewpoints too and that we, as readers, are not necessarily hearing about them.

Personal narrator: Amongst the titles, there are several stories which are told by a personal narrator. *Five Children and It* will surprise many readers as the story has scarcely started when E. Nesbit is speaking directly to us as the author of the story:

> Now that I have begun to tell you about the place, I feel that I could go on and make this into a most interesting story about all the ordinary things that the children did – just the kind of things you do yourself, you know.

Sometimes she even checks herself (with a degree of false modesty?):

> Lending ears was common in Roman times, as we learn from Shakespeare; but I fear I am getting too instructive.

This 'I' of course is not a character in the story and it takes some time to understand this literary convention. Perhaps exposure to the technique could be introduced early with *Harry, the Poisonous Centipede* in which Lynne Reid Banks not only intrudes but has interactive conversations with her readers:

> Harry lived in a very hot country – what we call the tropics – with his mother.
> Now, please don't start asking what *her* name was. Oh no. Please. Oh… All right. Here goes. It was Bkvllbbchk. Bikvilababchuk? Bokvaliboobchak? Bakvolobibchawk? I don't know. Why bother? We'll never get it right. Let's call her Belinda.

Not every reader likes such intrusion though it is interesting to see it in books which span nearly 100 years of writing for children.

A personal narrator can also be the author pretending to be autobiographical. Julian in *Julian, Dream Doctor* and Michael in *The Wreck of the Zanzibar* both tell their stories in the first person and readers are intended to assume that the events really happened to them. Similarly, Michael's great aunt Laura writes in the first person in her letter to Michael and in her diary account in *The Wreck of*

Teacher pages

the Zanzibar. Readers who are used to taking on role, either in their drama work in school or in their written activities find little problem with this first person narration. Often the pupil activities on the pupil pages (the right-hand pages) capitalise on the narrative voice and devices in a book such as this by asking pupils to write in a similar or related genre in role.

Further variations in personal narration come in the following two books. In *Celebration Song*, Mary, the mother of Jesus, speaks throughout the whole of the lyrical text, addressing it to her son and thus using the vocative 'you' throughout. In *The Stinky Cheese Man and Other Fairly Stupid Tales*, the first person narrator, Jack, is also the character Jack, who interacts with other characters (insulting their storytelling abilities rather recklessly, if the teller is the giant). Jack also interacts with us, his readers, instructing us, for instance to turn the pages quietly so that he can escape whilst the giant is sleeping. There is no doubt that this particular text challenges experienced readers but deconstructing its narrative voices and devices certainly helps and adds to the fun.

Very young or inexperienced readers, for whom the majority of books are written in the third person, are often puzzled by the first person 'I'. Reputedly, *Black Beauty* always helps in the sorting out of narrator and author: the first person narration is delivered by the horse!

Devices: The most extreme examples of narrative devices occur in *The Stinky Cheese Man and Other Fairly Stupid Stories* (see the teacher page, the left-hand page, for further details). In *Celebration Song* (and to some extent in *Storm*) there is a flashback to an earlier time. In *Storm* also and in *Children of Winter* there is a story-within-a-story. In *Children of Winter* this is in the form of a time-slip fantasy. In *The Great Elephant Chase* there are letters from Cissie which not only establish a period tone but also give a different viewpoint. As previously mentioned, *The Wreck of the Zanzibar* is predominantly in letter and diary form. *'The chicken gave it to me'* alternates one chapter from the chicken's book with one told by a third person narrator about the two children. The illustrator helpfully reminds us where we are by decorating the chicken's chapters with a three-toed hen's footprints. *The Firework-Maker's Daughter* has several narrative strands taking place contemporaneously. The author helps us cope with these parallel stories with a sprinkling of 'meanwhile' and 'by this time'.

The picture book illustrators are also inventive in their use of narrative devices. Charles Keeping uses the most effective device of moving his black and white illustrations into 'negatives' (in the photographic sense) for Bess and her highwayman's rendezvous after their deaths. Juan Wijngaard makes an understated link between the two women through the green girdle in *Sir Gawain and the Green Knight*. Louise Brierley's red rocks in the final opening of *Celebration Song* have powerful symbolic significance.

Theme Under this heading is given a brief and subjective opinion of the theme or themes that are discernible in each book. It is subjective because in this area particularly we make our own meanings. Themes in books are not necessarily transparent; writers do not state their themes overtly in the same way as they name characters, decide settings and send their plot through twists and turns. We have to distil the message according to our experience, our needs, our predilections. It is conceivable that one could read a book without making the theme explicit to oneself and indeed I suspect this is very common in childhood – though I like to think that significance can work at a subconscious level. On the whole, children's books emerge as concerned with issues to do with:

- overcoming fears
- greed
- encouraging generosity
- survival
- love and hate
- keeping and breaking promises
- rites of passage/growing up
- faith
- altruism
- maintaining relationships
- luck
- the getting of wisdom
- courage
- resilience
- honour
- good versus evil
- the use and misuse of magic
- understanding difference
- adjustment
- celebrating imagination
- self-sacrifice
- coping with new experiences.

There is much to discuss with pupils in terms of how they see the emerging 'point' of a book. It is less useful to ask 'What did you think the author's message was?' or 'Why do you think the author wrote this book?' – questions I certainly remember being asked as a school pupil. Themes are to do with making individual meaning. Let the children be the experts on this, and let them dispute the themes I have detected.

Characters Under this heading on the teacher pages, all the main characters' names are given, with some indication of their age (if relevant and known), their relationship to each other and their occupation or important characteristic.

Some characters are magical or not human: centipedes in *Harry, the Poisonous Centipede*, the Buccas in *Thomas and the Tinners*, the eponymous shape-changer in Julian Atterton's book and the Psammead in *Five Children and It*. Animal characters are included also, such as elephants – one realistic in *The Great Elephant Chase* and one magical in *The Firework-Maker's Daughter*; the troublesome gerbils in *The Battle of Bubble and Squeak*; the plucky chicken in *'The chicken gave it to me'* and the magical hare, Wiz, in *Harriet's Hare*.

Amongst the human characters, ten of the main characters are male, eight are female, and in the remaining six books male and female characters share the limelight. The characters in *Grace & Family* and *Julian, Dream Doctor* are of Afro-Caribbean origin; in *Celebration Song*, the illustrator gives us a black Mary and Jesus in a black community. Jazz in *Princess Jazz and the Angels* is of Irish/Punjabi descent and her Punjabi family are major players in the story. All the characters appear to be Indian or Indonesian in *The Firework-Maker's Daughter*. The ages of the main characters range from about eight (Julian) or nine (Grace in *Grace & Family* and Annie in *Storm*) to adult. The cast list in *The Shape-Changer*, *The Highwayman*, *The Pied Piper of Hamelin* and in *Sir Gawain and the Green Knight* is almost totally adult. This is something to consider if your class, group or individual pupil needs to be coaxed into reading books with no child characters. (For further comments on the age of characters, see under Titles and Levels of 'Difficulty' on page 7. On each teacher page, the characters' ages are given where they are known; otherwise approximate ages are given.

There is a range of main character types across the 24 books. Some, such as Thomas in *Thomas and the Tinners*, are essentially solid, innocent and good-natured; some, such as Grace in *Grace & Family* and Lila in *The Firework-Maker's Daughter* are spirited, imaginative and independent. Some are mischievous (Julian in *Julian, Dream Doctor* and Harry in *Harry, the Poisonous Centipede*) and Jazz in *Princess Jazz and the Angels* is bordering on incorrigible for much of the book. Many have to show great courage (Gawain in *Sir Gawain and the Green Knight*, all the children in *Children of Winter*, Kari in *The Shape-*

Teacher pages

Changer, Laura in *The Wreck of the Zanzibar* and Johanna in *The Little Riders*). All the characters in *Harvey Angell* are unusual and entertaining though not particularly complex. The brother and sister in *The Finding* are multi-faceted characters and they find themselves within an intricately plotted book, perhaps the most challenging title in this collection.

Some writers use their characters to challenge stereotypes. Margaretha Shemin counteracts much anti-German war material with her delicate portrait of Captain Braun. Grace's grandmother in *Grace & Family* is not only loving and wise but quite vigorous and trendy too (look at her dancing). The Major in *The Finding*, stereotyped initially through his speech, turns out to be the most sensitive questioner of Alex's sister Laura when Alex goes missing. The mother in *The Battle of Bubble and Squeak* is not what mothers are meant to be! She *hates* those gerbils for most of the book. Jazz's mother also upsets stereotypes by deserting her daughter at the beginning of the book. We have strong, brave girls in many narratives and less obviously dominant boys who are often very willing to give voice to their fears. Julian's dad is shown nearly sick with fear. The three visiting firework-makers from Germany, Italy and USA in *The Firework-Maker's Daughter* are absolute caricatures and as such are rather close to the bone. You and your pupils will decide if Philip Pullman has gone too far.

In nearly all the books the characters' particular natures contribute to the way the plot develops. Jerome Bruner (1986) rightly points out that elements of story do not rest only or even primarily upon action and interaction but upon character. He quotes Greimas, whose view is that an irreducible feature of story is that it occurs jointly on the plane of action and in the 'subjectivity of the protagonists'. Bruner calls this the 'dual landscape' of story. The way in which plot is derived from the working out of character in a particular setting is a focus of many of the suggested activities for pupils.

Setting As indicated, the setting of so much fiction is inextricable from plot and character. None of *The Great Elephant Chase* would be conceivable without the sense of the great river and the wide open plains of the prairie that permeate the book. Tad and Cissie's particular adventures are dictated by the constraints of setting as much as by their two natures.

It is tempting to speculate that a precise location is the start of many an author's and illustrator's narrative impulse. Imagine the Cornish tin mines and *Thomas and the Tinners* is almost written – well, perhaps not quite! Berlie Doherty acknowledges the pupils of a school where she was writer-in-residence who showed her the old cruck barn which is the location for so much of *Children of Winter*. We can tell from the notebook of Rachel Anderson how significant her visit to India was for the conception of *Jazz and the Angels* and, in this book, the settings (the Glasgow tenement flat, the foster-parents' home, the rural Punjabi home, the hospital, the Golden Temple of Amritsar) are easy to visualise. Pupils' attention is focused on setting in some of the activities in titles whose authors have achieved this.

Most of the picture books can teach important lessons about attending to setting. *Grace & Family*, *Sir Gawain and the Green Knight*, *Celebration Song* and *The Pied Piper of Hamelin* all encourage the interconnecting of character and plot with setting and, in addition, the illustrations add authentic geographic or period detail not so easy to imagine from words alone when you have not had much experience of reading. In *The Highwayman* we see some of Charles Keeping's skill at lending atmosphere through his exact line drawings: the road which winds like a ribbon and down which the lover must come is memorable.

It is not only the picture books however that owe a great deal to their illustrators in terms of the recreation of setting. Alan Marks is the illustrator of two books in this selection (*Storm* and *Thomas and the Tinners*) and his work and that of Christian Birmingham in *The Wreck of the Zanzibar* adds depth, interest and atmosphere to the books. Quentin Blake is frequently Joan Aiken's accompanist as in *The Winter Sleepwalker* and well suited to each other's sparky talents they are too. Philippe Dupasquier (*'The chicken gave it to me'*) and Tony Ross (*Harry, the Poisonous Centipede*) are aptly chosen for the humorous books they illustrate and Peter Spier adds fine Dutch detail to *The Little Riders*.

Where the time of year is significant, details are given under this heading. The depiction of bitter winter or of violent storms is part of the atmosphere of *Storm*, *Children of Winter*, *The Little Riders*, *Sir Gawain and the Green Knight* and *The Wreck of the Zanzibar* just as the feel of long, hot summer days permeates *Julian, Dream Doctor*, *Harriet's Hare* and *Five Children and It*. In several books, the season is irrelevant and thus no reference is made to it.

Era Ten of the books in this selection of two dozen are set in the present day. The remainder cover the following span:

World War II: *The Little Riders*

Around 1900: *Thomas and the Tinners*, *The Wreck of the Zanzibar*, *The Great Elephant Chase* and *Five Children and It*

Early 18th century: *The Highwayman*

1665: *Children of Winter*

14th century: *Sir Gawain and the Green Knight*, *The Pied Piper of Hamelin*

Around 842: *The Shape-Changer*

1 AD: *Celebration Song*.

The remaining three books, *The Winter Sleepwalker*, *The Firework-Maker's Daughter* and *The Stinky Cheese Man and Other Fairly Stupid Stories*, are set in a timeless or fantasy time, though all reveal that their authors are very much of this day and age.

It is stated in the National Curriculum that children should read some long-established children's fiction. Perforce, this means that children should read about an era which is not 'our' present day. *Five Children and It* was written about the 'then' present day of 1902. To adults, of course, this book captures the period feel successfully. To many children, a book such as *The Wreck of the Zanzibar*, written in the present day but about the same period in history as *Five Children and It*, can carry just as much or even more conviction about the era and life in the time. And of course, we are dependent on writers *not* of the time to make available to young readers fiction set in, for instance, the plague years or Viking times.

Language Figurative: Under this heading, where relevant, is given an indication with examples of the author's use of simile, metaphor, alliteration, onomatopoeia, personification, idioms, puns and other rhetorical devices. On the pupil page for *Harvey Angell*, there is a brief explanation for pupils of some of these terms. The authors represented here who employ figurative language to sparkling effect are

Ann Cameron, Kevin Crossley-Holland, Joan Aiken, Michael Morpurgo, Diana Hendry, Berlie Doherty, and the two poets Alfred Noyes and Robert Browning. It often comes as a surprise that rather little figurative language is used by a poet such as James Berry in the unusual *Celebration Song* or by Rachel Anderson in her vigorous *Princess Jazz and the Angels*. Both of these authors write in distinctive ways yet their use of conventional devices is minimal. In fact, several of the writers in this selection use very little figurative language and create books with a clean or hard-edged feel about them which suits the story.

I think pupils need to realise that an author writes in a particular way (imagine Joan Aiken without her rich language) after years of developing a style to suit her- or himself. One of the associated hazards of exercises which isolate figurative language is that pupils feel that similes = good, no similes = bad, which results in mechanical or forced language. One of the strengths of the writing represented here is that the figurative language used is so unaffected and grows from the subject matter of the story. A place to start looking at the organic nature of effective use of figurative language might be Kevin Crossley-Holland's *Storm*.

Use of standard/dialect: Very few of the books make any use of dialect except in dialogue. An inspection of the way dialect is used and of its written representation could be fruitfully made from the following books: *Princess Jazz and the Angels*, *The Finding*, '*The chicken gave it to me*', *Harriet's Hare*, *Five Children and It*, *Children of Winter*, *Thomas and the Tinners* and *The Great Elephant Chase*. Many pupils enjoy reading aloud these parts of books and making attempts to write dialogue in dialect themselves. Teachers can develop their own activities to support such work and for some of the books above specific tasks are suggested.

Use of direct speech: Most children's authors seem to respond to Alice in Wonderland's famous question: 'What is the point of a book without pictures or conversations?' at least as far as the dialogue is concerned. Some readers need help with long tracts of narrative unbroken by speech and on the whole few books in this list are written this way. Perhaps one of the reasons that Anne Fine and Dick King-Smith are such popular writers for young people is the inclusion of so much dialogue in their books. Both are skilled at moving the story on through talk and thoughts. Both are skilled at capturing realistic speech. Even the speech of the children in E. Nesbit's book is immediate and accessible to readers nearly 100 years later. Nina Bawden is noted for her ability to convey character through speech and Diana Hendry's spirited dialogue is a major strength in *Harvey Angell*, contributing undoubtedly to the fact that the book is under consideration for a film.

Activities are included which encourage pupils to work on dialogue. Wherever there is a long section in a book without speech or without interiorising on a character's part, there is usually a chance for teachers to ask readers to imagine what would have been said or thought.

Other: Under this heading are diverse observations about the author's language. Sometimes the use of rhyme or song is worth recording as in *Thomas and the Tinners* or *The Winter Sleepwalker*. The inclusion of quotations from other books, as in *Julian, Dream Maker* or '*The chicken gave it to me*' is also mentioned here. Under this heading, I have also recorded the existence of technical, archaic, invented and compound words, and colloquial, formal, obscure or unexpected vocabulary. In books set in the past (*The Great Elephant Chase*, *The Wreck of the Zanzibar*, *Thomas and the Tinners*, *Sir Gawain and the Green Knight*) the author may have tried to capture the rhythms and structures of the language of the time, and this is noted. *Five Children and It* and the Noyes and Browning poems were written in the past and their particular language features are isolated. Attention is brought to books where the language is effectively simple and clean-edged, appropriate to the type of story, as in *The Shape-Changer*, and where complex concepts are expressed simply as in *The Finding*.

The poems in the list are mostly poems that tell a story but in all cases their language is worthy of inspection. Under this heading and also in the pupil activities children are encouraged to deal with aspects of language use such as reversed word order, alliteration, rhyme, including half-rhymes, ellipsis and patterning. The imagery of the poems is usually referred to under the heading Figurative Language. Children are often more sensitive towards features than we expect and occasionally activities are suggested that start with a reading aloud or in the preparation of a reading to others. This is an activity that can be used for all poetry.

Story structure

This section includes story summaries which are approached in a different way from conventional reviews where the reader must not be told too much. The intentions here are to give teachers an opportunity to check whether this book appeals to them and would appeal to their pupils; to refresh their memory of the book; and, particularly, to aid them in an analysis of the story structure.

Traditionally story structure has received little attention in classrooms but recently the genre theorists, in conjunction with analysts of 'story grammars', psychologists and sociologists, have given more emphasis to the elements of story and their functions. Beginning, middle and end is a start but we need a more fine-tuned breakdown.

The 'opening': This may include important details of the time, place and participants. Labov (1972) calls this the 'orientation' which is a helpful term; Bruner (1986) calls it the 'state of equilibrium' and Longacre (1983) the 'exposition'.

Often, inexperienced readers find the 'opening' difficult to read as it contains so much information and little action. Teachers often read the opening paragraphs to a class or put them on to tape in order to help children into the book. Many authors (an example in this selection is Dick King-Smith) weave informative details into the fabric of the text *after* beginning with dramatic action which is properly the 'inciting' moment (see below).

The 'inciting moment': This is when things start to happen. This term (Longacre's) is not easy to use with children perhaps but is better than 'crisis' (which has too much association with calamity) or 'problem' (which often seems too minor). Bruner uses the term 'breach', Labov 'complicating action' and Todorov (1977) 'disruption'. Experienced readers can usually detect when the story takes this turn; the traditional tale breaks into the earlier scene-setting with words like 'one day' or 'now it happened that...'.

The 'development': At this point the action becomes more involved. Within the development there may be further crises, developments, climaxes and solutions.

The 'denouement': This is Longacre's term and describes when a final event occurs making resolution possible and when we, as readers, sense the ending coming up. Labov uses the term 'resolution' for this part in the narrative and thus needs the term 'coda' for the final stage.

The 'ending': Also known as 'redress' (Bruner's term), 'reinstatement' (Todorov) or 'conclusion' (Longacre), this brings the conflict to a satisfactory resolution. There is never a simple return to the opening status quo; the characters are always changed. Often the theme of the book may become clinched here.

The National Curriculum (influenced by the unpublished LINC materials which explored these areas) has played its part in emphasising story structure. The evidence is that viewing stories in this way certainly interests children and gives them a control which feeds their appreciation of books and helps shape their own writing.

The author and illustrator Under this heading the briefest relevant information is given. The intention is simply to indicate whether the authors and illustrators are still living, their chief claims to fame, their better known titles and a note of any biographical aspects of interest, including any awards won.

Teachers may want their pupils to investigate authors and illustrators further. Useful sources of reference include the following.

- The journal, *Books for Keeps*, has useful interviews called 'Authorgraphs' in the centre pages of all issues.

- *Treasure Islands 2* (Rosen and Burridge, 1993) has lively author profiles.

- Various guides to children's literature have short entries, for example *The Oxford Companion to Children's Literature* (Carpenter and Pritchard, 1984).

- Publishers will sometimes provide information and major book shops produce inexpensive guides with brief summaries of authors, such as *Waterstones' Guide to Children's Books*.

Activities In the space available on the teacher page, I have indicated what the pupil activities are designed to enable, develop and promote. Different titles are accompanied by different activities; the aims also have different focal points based on the particular strengths of the book. Overall, however, the aims are guided by a belief that a dynamic engagement with books enables all of us to widen our horizons and understand the world better. The National Curriculum, which I have taken seriously on this point, wants our pupils to develop 'as enthusiastic, independent and reflective readers' which are aims no-one would oppose. I have also heeded the Key Skills for Key Stage 2 which, in brief, are that:

> pupils should be taught to consider in detail the quality and depth of what they read. They should be encouraged to respond imaginatively to the plot, characters, ideas, vocabulary and organisation of language in literature. They should be taught to use inference and deduction ... and to evaluate the texts they read, and to refer to relevant passages to support their opinions.

By developing activities based on a book, these aims may be realised; regrettably, they may also be hindered and it is my fervent wish that the activities do not become a chore for pupils. I trust teachers to be selective, shrewd and flexible when it comes to their own pupils and to allow reading to be unaccompanied by written work on occasions.

As teachers, we *are* hoping to support pupils in close reading, in deeper reflection, in appreciation and analysis of the author's techniques, in the extraction of information, and in appreciation of the achievement. The ways in which these aims are achieved are various and many of them can be achieved through discussion.

The emphasis in the activities in the pupil pages is more on written activities than on talk, not because talk is not essential – before, during and after – but because talk is more likely to arise from personal pupil and teacher concerns which are not predictable by an outsider. I *have* indicated several activities for talk but *every* book lends itself to discussion and all teachers will want to have talk time as a regular activity. For good talk sessions around books, there is no short-cut: teachers must know the books well, ask thoughtful questions and then attend closely to the children's responses, not pre-empting their ideas. For guidance and inspiration for talking with children about their reading and books, I cannot recommend Aidan Chambers' book *Tell Me* (1983) highly enough.

The pupil pages are divided into sections A, B, C and D in order to separate different aims.

Assessment Through teacher and self-evaluation of the work, there are opportunities to make quite formal assessments of pupils' achievements. The following is a list of what the activities can enable teachers to assess. Each separate book's activities yield only a few of these opportunities. It is sensible for instance to focus on language work with a text that is more highly wrought (perhaps *Harvey Angell*) than one where the language is relatively unadorned. The major skills that may emerge when looking at children's work on the activities include the ability to:

- present ideas succinctly (*Harvey Angell*)
- tell a story, retaining key points (*The Shape-Changer, The Little Riders, The Stinky Cheese Man and Other Fairly Stupid Tales*)
- ask and answer questions in role (*The Shape-Changer*)
- read between the lines (*The Shape-Changer*)
- express characters' unspoken thoughts (inference and deduction) (*The Shape-Changer, Princess Jazz and the Angels, Children of Winter*)
- create a further story (*The Shape-Changer*)
- show response to setting and style (*The Shape-Changer*)
- base predictions on close reading (*Storm, The Pied Piper of Hamelin, Children of Winter*)
- offer evaluative comment (*Storm, Celebration Song, The Winter Sleepwalker*)
- identify relevant factual information (*Harry, the Poisonous Centipede, Sir Gawain and the Green Knight, The Great Elephant Chase*)
- track the events of the plot (*Harry, the Poisonous Centipede, The Battle of Bubble and Squeak, The Wreck of the Zanzibar*)
- use language in specific ways, modelled on the author's use (*Harry, the Poisonous Centipede, The Firework-Maker's Daughter, Harvey Angell*)
- perceive how character, emotion and plot are interdependent (*Harry, the Poisonous Centipede, The Battle of Bubble and Squeak, The Great Elephant Chase*)
- write a character study based on information in the text (*'The chicken gave it to me', The Little Riders*)
- identify argument (*'The chicken gave it to me'*)

- detect how a book is structured (*Harriet's Hare, Five Children and It, Children of Winter, The Great Elephant Chase*)
- pick up clues and fill in the 'telling gaps' (*Harriet's Hare, The Highwayman*)
- read beyond the text (*Harriet's Hare*) and carry out research (*The Stinky Cheese Man and Other Fairly Stupid Tales*)
- analyse illustrations (*The Little Riders, Sir Gawain and the Green Knight, The Highwayman*)
- convey understanding through a prepared reading (*Celebration Song, The Highwayman, The Firework-Maker's Daughter*)
- imagine a character's feelings (*Sir Gawain and the Green Knight, The Pied Piper of Hamelin, The Finding*)
- write in verse (*Celebration Song*)
- detect deeper significance (*The Battle of Bubble and Squeak, The Finding*)
- appreciate the writer's style (*The Winter Sleepwalker, The Firework-Maker's Daughter*)
- write a story or extra scene (*The Winter Sleepwalker, The Stinky Cheese Man and Other Fairly Stupid Tales, The Firework-Maker's Daughter, Children of Winter*)
- read poetry with attention to the metre (*The Highwayman*)
- scan text (*Princess Jazz and the Angels, The Stinky Cheese Man and Other Fairly Stupid Tales, Children of Winter*)
- visualise settings (*Princess Jazz and the Angels, The Great Elephant Chase*)
- discuss feelings (*The Pied Piper of Hamelin*)
- critically evaluate (*The Wreck of the Zanzibar, Five Children and It, The Firework-Maker's Daughter, Children of Winter, The Finding*)
- write additional dialogue (*The Wreck of the Zanzibar, Children of Winter*)
- discuss in groups (several titles)
- re-write key scenes (*The Wreck of the Zanzibar*)
- debate moral issues (*Five Children and It, The Finding, 'The chicken gave it to me'*)
- add illustrations or ideas for illustrations (*The Stinky Cheese Man and Other Fairly Stupid Tales, The Little Riders*)
- recreate description (*The Firework-Maker's Daughter*)
- summarise (*Harvey Angell*)
- refer to relevant passages when offering views (*The Finding*).

In addition, because of the format which many of the activities encourage, there should be evidence that pupils have the ability to:

- read aloud
- write a story

- subvert a story
- write an information file
- make maps and plans
- invent new words, using knowledge of parts of speech
- ask and answer questions in role
- read an obituary
- write letters of various types to both real and imaginary audiences
- write lists
- write tourist brochures
- write diary entries
- write an information book entry
- consult a dictionary
- write a social worker's report
- write a scene from a play
- write a prayer
- write resolutions
- write notes for a film script
- create a poster
- write a book review
- write a reference for a character
- write notes
- write and conduct interviews
- contribute to all elements of a newspaper
- make a board game
- evaluate statements.

Related reading The books mentioned briefly at the end of every teacher page are related to the title in many different ways, not all of which are made explicit. Another book may have a similar theme but it may present difficulties that were not present in the original book or it may be much 'easier'. Nearly all the 'war' titles are considerably more complex than *The Little Riders* with which they are linked. *Shaker Lane* has era and one aspect – Shakers – in common with *The Great Elephant Chase* but is in fact a much simpler picture book. I may suggest a title by the same author but thematically there will be no link (all Philip Pullman's novels, for instance, are very different). Some of the links are personal and tenuous. There is really no short-cut here; teachers have to make their own judgements, after reading the books, on relevance and suitability.

Pupil pages

On these pages I address the pupils directly. The pages are photocopiable. Occasionally, pupils are asked to complete charts on the actual photocopied sheet – if preferred, they can be asked to copy out the chart.

I have not suggested how the books are to be read. They all lend themselves to being read aloud by the teacher or by competent readers; equally, all lend themselves to private reading.

The advantages of whole-class reading are numerous. The evidence is clear that it promotes more reading, that it provides pupils with the 'tune on the page', that it brings complex books within the reach of all the class. The feeling of the entire class knowing the same book, of creating a whole-class shared culture, is exciting and worth working carefully to create. If the teacher intends to do prediction activities (whilst looking at the cover, or after reading the blurb or the first few pages or chapters), it is useful to work with the whole class initially to control the activity more effectively.

All the books could be used for group reading if enough copies are available. The advantages here are also considerable, with more precise matching of group interests and needs being possible and more opportunity for pupils to work collaboratively.

All the books can be given to individuals who are able to manage them. The importance of sustained silent reading needs no special pleading here. We all want children to know the experience of being lost in a book. However not all the activities can be done alone nor would that be desirable so bringing a pair or group of silent readers together for discussion, drama and writing is important.

There are expectations that the pupils will be working in various *different* combinations: singly, in pairs, in groups, with the whole class. The teacher will need to check individual activities and assess which grouping is most suitable.

On occasions, the activities can be attempted before or during reading the particular book. This is specified where, for instance, prediction activities are to be carried out.

The activities are divided into sections A, B, C and D. There is always a change of focus from one activity to another and generally the activities increase in complexity. If they do not, it is still important to consider whether change in the order of undertaking may create problems.

My guiding philosophy used when preparing these activities needs to be read in conjunction with the comments given under Aims.

On the whole, I believe that there are three major ways in which pupils achieve our aims satisfactorily. They achieve our aims when:

- we respect their own experience and we encourage the linking of book themes with their first-hand experience. This can be done effectively before the book is read (see the activity in *The Pied Piper of Hamelin*) and is on the whole an approach (often called brainstorming) well understood by teachers, partly because pupils show us the way. Their natural inclination to make texts relevant to themselves is very apparent. Talking in pairs, groups and in whole-class discussion is the major way of promoting the deepening of understanding and response that teachers want to achieve.

- we show them how to do it. For this reason I frequently offer a model for pupils to reflect upon. They 'see' what is expected of them and they feel confident to attempt the task. This is not making life too easy for them; it is more to do with working in their 'zone of proximal development', to use Vygotsky's (1978) over-quoted but illuminating phrase. So often, pupils do not receive models and then we are disappointed with their results. By offering an example – whether by filling in the first line of a chart or by offering other views as a start for pupils' writing of their own reviews – we stimulate, clarify and support, and pupils' work benefits.

- we offer them purposeful activities. I have made most of the activities take the form of 'real' writing or speaking tasks. They are not exercises or questions which ask for simple factual recall.

We have all come a long way in our understanding of how much more readily children write and how much more they achieve when they are writing or talking:

- for **purposes** to which they can relate

- for **audiences** which they can visualise or imagine

- in **forms** of which they have seen counterparts in real life.

The National Writing Project has provided much evidence of the truth of this and the original National Curriculum (the 'Cox' curriculum) helped teachers greatly with its 'Approaches to the Class Novel', to which readers should refer for further ideas.

One of the results of these three guiding principles is that the activities take longer to explain than traditional tasks. I hope the compensations are clear and that pupils begin to feel that the demands on their reading stamina are worth it when they realise that the support and focus enable them to get on with an enjoyable and understandable assignment. If the pupils *do* find that they lose their way in reading long outlines of activities, there is no reason why teachers shouldn't work through the various elements with the class.

Pupil response sheets

There are six photocopiable sheets which can be used with these books and, with a little adaptation, with any books that individuals read. The aims of these pages are not only to do with record keeping – though they effectively accomplish that – but to do with structuring responses.

1 Reading record (page 26)	This sheet reminds pupils of the need to read and re-read and of the importance of the contexts in which they read.
2 The cover and illustrations (page 27)	This sheet takes pupils through an appraisal of the visual aspects of the book, aiding both recall and evaluation. It offers pupils the chance to reflect on alternative and/or additional illustrations.
3 The story (page 28)	Pupils are aided in their reflection on story, story structure, predictions and memories.
4 The characters (page 29)	Pupils are supported in their recollections of character development and relationships.
5 Setting and **The language of the book** (page 30)	This sheet is in two sections. **Setting** helps pupils appreciate how author and illustrator set the book in time and place. **The language of the book** gives pupils the chance to record challenges and felicities in the language of the book.
6 Themes and **Activities** (page 31)	This sheet is also in two sections. **Themes** gives the opportunity for pupils to record their understanding of each book's impact on them. **Activities** gives space for the pupil to make a record of activities undertaken, with whom and with what result. A final space allows for a recommendation.

On the whole, pupils enjoy the completion of sheets such as these; they echo the typical responses to reading literature, following through such processes as anticipating, picturing, reflecting back, making connections and evaluating. However, it would be a mistake to insist on completion of all six sheets for every book read if they are not seen as useful and interesting to all concerned.

Conclusion

I am relieved that the National Curriculum has got so much right about literature teaching. It understands about range – stories, plays, poetry, picture books. It understands that children need the familiar and the unfamiliar, the imaginary and the fantastic. It has a quite proper regard for the elements of plot, character and setting. It wants us to enjoy language. It knows that considerable enjoyment comes from books where authors leave us to deduce and infer – the work we do to 'fill in the gaps' is always rewarding and pleasurable. It understands that we must read to our classes not just hear them read; that we need to talk with them about stories and what will happen next. It understands about re-reading, the importance of guidance and of own choice.

However the National Curriculum has not, in its present form, helped very much with bringing about this enjoyment of and respect for literature. There has been little practical help in the actual *teaching*, and other areas of the National Curriculum have, as I have said, squeezed out much reading of and writing about literature. This seems particularly regrettable when we have so many rich and wondrous books written for children.

Is there a wind of change blowing? Are we realising, anew, that none of us can do without narrative? For many, literature is the area of the curriculum that gives pleasure, that enables emotional, social, aesthetic and moral development to take place, that informs and delights in equal measure. Through literature, we explore new, different and diverse worlds. We can become many people as we read; we can envisage our futures.

It is important that teachers stay enthusiastic. If the books chosen here and the activities for pupils preserve enthusiasm, this book will serve its purpose.

References

Bruner, J. (1986) *Actual Minds, Possible Worlds* Cambridge, Massachusetts: Harvard University Press

Carpenter, H. and Pritchard, M. (1984) *The Oxford Companion to Children's Literature* Oxford: Oxford University Press

Chambers, A. (1983) *Tell Me: Children, Reading and Talk* South Woodchester: The Thimble Press

DES (1989) *English for ages 5 to 16* (The Cox Report) London: HMSO

DFE (1995) *The National Curriculum* London: HMSO

HMI (1990) *The Teaching and Learning of Reading in Primary Schools: A Report* London: HMSO

Labov, W. (1972) *Language in the Inner-City* Philadelphia: University of Pennsylvania Press

Longacre, R. E. (1983) *The Grammar of Discourse* New York and London: Plenum

Rosen, M. and Burridge, J. (1993) *Treasure Islands 2* London: BBC Books

SCDC (1990) *The National Writing Project* – various theme packs and in-service materials. Walton-on-Thames: Thomas Nelson

Todorov, T. (1977) *The Poetics of Fiction* Oxford: Blackwell

Vygotsky, L. (1978) *Mind in Society* Cambridge, Massachusetts: Harvard University Press

Journal

Books for Keeps (6 issues a year) School Bookshop Association, 6, Brightfield Road, Lee, London SE12 8QF

1 Reading record

Name: .... **Date:** ....

Title of book: ....

The author:
_____

The illustrator:
_____

Date I started reading (the first time):
_____

Date I finished reading (the first time):
_____

Date I started reading (the second time):
_____

Date I finished reading (the second time):
_____

Any further times read?
_____

How I read the book (with a group, silently, listening to the teacher, at home, etc.):
_____
_____

Which pages (if any) I read aloud:
_____
_____

Name: .... **Date:** ....

Title of book: ....

2 The cover and illustrations

What I thought when I saw the cover of the book:

_____

_____

_____

Now that I have read the book, my opinion of the cover:

_____

_____

My ideas for an alternative cover:

Name of illustrator:

_____

What I thought of the illustrations. (If your book is unillustrated, write about whether you would have liked illustrations):

_____

_____

_____

What extra or different illustrations could there be?

_____

_____

_____

CRACKING GOOD BOOKS © *Judith Graham* 1997

Name: .... **Date:** ....

Title of book: ....

3
The story

What I thought was the moment when the story really began:

_____
_____
_____
_____
_____

What predictions I had about what was going to happen:

_____
_____
_____
_____
_____

What did happen:

_____
_____
_____
_____
_____

The part of the story that I remember most clearly:

_____
_____
_____
_____
_____

CRACKING GOOD BOOKS © *Judith Graham 1997*

Name: .... **Date:** ....

Title of book: ....

4
The characters

The main character's name:

Other important characters' names:

How the main character has changed by the end of the book:

How the main character's relationship with one or more of the other characters has changed by the end of the book:

CRACKING GOOD BOOKS © *Judith Graham* 1997

Name: .... **Date:** ....

Title of book: ....

5 Setting

Where the book I have read is set:

In what period of time my book is set (modern day, fantasy time, 1666, etc.):

Some of the details that helped me to visualise the setting, the people's clothes, the date of the story:

The language of the book

My favourite expressions in the book:

Words that I guessed the meaning of in the book:

Words that I had to look up or ask the meaning of in the book:

Figurative language that I enjoyed in the book:

The funniest thing anyone said in the book:

Name: .... Date: ....

Title of book: ....

6 Themes

What I think I have understood from reading this book:

_____
_____
_____
_____
_____

Activities

The activities (section and number) I have worked on with this book are (I have ticked those I have finished and I have written the names of the people I worked with or talked to about my work):

_____
_____
_____

The one I enjoyed doing most was:

_____

because:

_____
_____

The one I enjoyed doing least was:

_____

because:

_____

Recommendation to another reader

I think you would enjoy reading this book because:

_____
_____

1 Julian, Dream Doctor

by Ann Cameron
Illustrated by Ann Strugnell
First published by Random House, USA, 1990; in UK by Victor Gollancz, 1992; in paperback by Yearling, 1994
ISBN 0 440 86315 5

Genre	Biographical situation comedy
Narrative voice	First person story told by Julian
Theme	Surprises, generosity, overcoming fears
Characters	Julian, aged about 8, his younger brother Huey approximately 6, his father and mother, his friend Gloria
Setting	Not specified, but probably the Caribbean or the USA
Era	Present day
Language	Figurative: Plentiful similes: 'quiet as a turtle at the bottom of the sea'. Some metaphors: 'snakes are living neckties'
	Use of standard/dialect: Standard throughout
	Use of direct speech: A balance of dialogue and prose
	Other: Some 'Dalek' talk. Some quotation from an information book on snakes. Huey stutters when afraid.
Story structure	**Opening:** Julian introduces us to his family. His father's birthday is coming up. Julian longs to give his father a 'present which he had always dreamed of' but, despite his subtle attempts, he fails to draw from his father any practical ideas.
	Inciting moment: With his brother and Gloria, Julian questions his father whilst he is asleep in the hammock (in the belief that he can be prompted into truth-telling sleep-talking). His father murmurs something about snakes.
	Development: The trio, with some trepidation on the boys' part, catch two live snakes and parcel them up. The party has a snake party theme which unnerves their father somewhat. When he opens his present, he runs from the room.
	Denouement: Father reveals that snakes are his biggest fear.
	Ending: Taking heart from Julian's own experience when catching the snakes, father learns to overcome his fear and touches the snakes and blows out his birthday candles.
The author	Ann Cameron is American, known mostly in this country for her 'Julian' stories (see below).
The illustrator	Ann Strugnell is a British illustrator who has contributed soft pencil drawings of black children to several American books.
Activities	• Section A focuses on particularly imaginative, or telling moments of the text. The activities aim to give pupils opportunities to draw on first-hand experience; • Section B uncovers some of the depths in the story; • Section C gives children a chance to review the book.
Assessment	The ability to: • respond imaginatively with their own first-person account; • make the implicit more explicit; • select enjoyable aspects of the book and assess the book's appeal.
Related reading	Ann Cameron and Ann Strugnell's earlier *The Julian Stories*, *More Stories Julian Tells* and *Julian, Secret Agent*; *My Naughty Little Sister* by Dorothy Edwards

CRACKING GOOD BOOKS

1 Julian, Dream Doctor

by **Ann Cameron**
Illustrated by Ann Strugnell
Page references are to the Yearling 1994 paperback edition.

A *While reading the book*

1 *Read the first three chapters.* When Julian and Huey are trying to find out from their father what he likes more than anything else in the world he says, 'You and Huey and Mum' and 'the ocean' and 'mountains' and 'an atom' and 'a star'. All of them are 'awfully hard to wrap' as Huey says. Write a list of things you like more than anything else in the world that are also hard to wrap.

2 *Read the fourth chapter.* Julian tries to pick up signals from his father's brain to find out what he wants as a present. He sets up a machine in the garden made of what Huey calls 'stuff' and he holds on to the TV aerial to receive a message. Neither works. In your group, share ideas of other crazy (or not so crazy) ways in which Julian and Huey could try to get the information out of their father.

3 *Read the fifth chapter.* The children are sure that they've got the information about his dream present out of their sleeping father. They very sensibly use a book about snakes to help them catch safe ones and, when they are successful, they are 'amazed, amazed, amazed' at overcoming their fear. What fears have you overcome? Write an account of when you were pleased that you overcame a fear.

4 *After reading the book.* Now you know what Julian's father was dreaming about and how he came to get snakes as his 'dream present'. Do you dream? In your group, share memories of dreams you have had. You may also want to write about one.

B 5 This story is told by Julian. He is the narrator and it is often very obvious that he feels he is older and wiser than Huey. He does not tell us this in so many words however. Look at the following pages and find the lines which tell us that Julian feels more grown up than Huey.

Pages 11, 18–19, 25, 39, 46, 48–49, 68

Now find the lines which tell us that Huey is also quite clever.

Pages 27, 29, 38, 46

6 At the beginning, Julian imagined his father saying 'Julian, you're a genius! This is the most unforgettable birthday that I have ever had.' Now that you have finished the book, do you think his father would still say that?

Can you now explain the title, *Julian, Dream Doctor*? Talk about it together.

C 7 Many children particularly like the illustrations in this book. Others like the crazy situations and the jokes. What do you like best? Give good reasons for what you say (or write).

CRACKING GOOD BOOKS © Judith Graham 1997

2
Thomas and the Tinners

by Jill Paton Walsh

Illustrated by Alan Marks

First published by Macdonald Young Books, 1995
ISBN
0 7500 1533 0

Genre	Short novel in six chapters, a mix of historical reality and fantasy
Narrative voice	Third person
Theme	Generosity rewarded and increasing maturity
Characters	Thomas, aged about 14, called Prentice Jack; other workers, all 'Jacks'; the ferryman, his wife and his daughter, Birdy; the magic little people in the mine, the Buccas
Setting	The coastal, tin mining country of Cornwall and down the mines
Era	19th century, towards the end of prosperity in the tin mines
Language	Figurative: Occasional vivid similes: a pasty 'as thick as a mattress'
	Use of standard/dialect: Mostly standard but with some Cornish dialect in the direct speech (see **section B**)
	Use of direct speech: a balanced mixture of description and dialogue
	Other: The Buccas address Thomas with a rhyme. Archaic expressions and technical terms to do with tin mining (see **section B**)
Story structure	Opening: Every morning the tin miners buy pasties from the ferryman's family, before they are rowed across the river mouth to the mine. Thomas, the new apprentice, is given a small pasty.
	Inciting moment: After a gruelling morning in the mine, Thomas sits down to eat but is greatly surprised by a tiny Bucca who is hungry. Thomas takes pity, his pasty is eaten and Thomas is granted his first wish (that it was home time).
	Development: On the next two mornings, Birdy gives Thomas a bigger and bigger pasty but on both days it is eaten by the Buccas and Thomas is given a wish in return, which he more or less wastes.
	Denouement: Thomas reveals to the ferryman's family what is happening to the pasties. He also hears of the miners' difficulties in finding more tin seams. An enormous pasty is cooked and carried to the mine in a wheelbarrow. The Buccas eat the pasty and Thomas at last wishes sensibly for more tin. The Buccas lead him to a rich lode.
	Ending: The miners' fortunes are made. Thomas becomes a rich man but he always returns to thank the Buccas with a huge pasty cooked by Birdy.
The author	Jill Paton Walsh lives in Cambridge, and has written many books, mostly for older children and adults. She is particularly well known for historical fiction such as *Grace*, the story of Grace Darling.
The illustrator	Alan Marks has contributed to several books including *Storm* (see page 40 of *Cracking Good Books*) and two volumes of Mother Goose rhymes.
Activities	• Section A sharpens predictions by drawing the pupils' attention to the features of a traditional story. • Section B allows children to reflect on and use some of the distinctive language of the book and to extend the story imaginatively.
Assessment	The ability to: • base prediction on recognition of common features of traditional tales; • re-tell a story; • detect and use linguistic style of book; • enter imaginatively into an extension of the story.
Related reading	By the same team, *Birdy and the Ghosties* and *Matthew and the Sea Singer*.

2 Thomas and the Tinners

by Jill Paton **Walsh**
Illustrated by Alan Marks

A 1 *Read up to the end of chapter 2.* Now talk with your partner, group or teacher about what you think will happen next. If you are reading alone, jot down your prediction on paper. The following questions will help you sharpen your prediction.

   a) What does Thomas feel about his first morning at work? Are you sorry for him?

   b) Why do you think only Thomas can hear and see the Bucca?

   c) Is Thomas sorry for the Bucca? Does he willingly offer his pasty to him?

   d) Do you think Thomas could have made a better wish?

   e) What often happens in tales where one wish is granted?

   f) Now look back at your prediction. Do you want to change it at all?

   2 *Now finish the story.* Talk with others who have read it also. Were you close in your idea of what would happen? This story has a very traditional shape which makes it a good one to learn and tell to others. See if you can re-tell it (after re-reading and practice).

B 3 Look again at the words the Buccas speak when they stop Thomas eating the pasty.

> Not so fast!
> Not so hasty!
> Give us a bite of that there pasty!
> We be mortal hungry!
> We be a-dying down here!

You will notice that it has a strong rhythm and a rhyme. It also uses some Cornish dialect and old-fashioned expressions.

Imagine that each time the adult Thomas takes a pasty to the Buccas they leave him a letter, written in true Bucca style. Write the rhyming letter. You may want to write more than one – perhaps Thomas might send a note with the pasties and you could write his letters too. Here is one Bucca letter written by a reader:

> Thomas we be waiting!
> Thomas we be pined.
> Not for the pasty
> On which we all have dined.
> But we want you to be wed
> To that there Birdy on the shore.
> You know that she's a likely lass
> So what you a-waiting for?

You can use expressions from the book or make up your own.

CRACKING GOOD BOOKS © *Judith Graham 1997* 35

3 Grace & Family

by Mary Hoffman
Illustrated by Caroline Binch
First published by Frances Lincoln, 1995; in paperback by Frances Lincoln, 1997
ISBN 0-7112-0869-7

Genre	Family story, picture book
Narrative voice	Third person, omniscient, impersonal narrator
Theme	New experiences, new wisdom
Characters	Grace, aged about 9; Mother; Nana; Father; Jatou, father's second wife; Neneh and Bakary, Grace's half-sister and half-brother
Setting	Predominantly in The Gambia, Africa
Era	Present day
Language	Figurative: One striking simile: 'I feel like gum all stretched out thin'
	Use of standard/dialect: Standard throughout
	Use of direct speech: Plenty
	Other: Complex emotions, very accessibly expressed
Story structure	Opening: Grace lives with her Ma and Nana but longs to live with her father as children in stories do. Her Nana points out that 'families are what you make them'.
	Inciting moment: Father sends two tickets for Grace and Nana to visit him and his new family in The Gambia.
	Development: Nana and Grace arrive in The Gambia and Grace feels a happy memory of her father returning. But when she meets his new family, Grace is uncertain that she is really wanted. She is wary of her stepmother, knowing, from stories, that stepmothers are not to be trusted. Her father helps her to change her attitude. Nana also helps her to come to terms with her extended family. She begins to enjoy the new experiences Africa has to offer and Neneh and Bakary hear lots of her stories.
	Denouement: At the holy crocodile enclosure, Grace makes a private wish.
	Ending: Grace resolves to write a story about her family who 'live happily ever after but not all in the same place'.
The author	Mary Hoffman is the author of over 40 books for children and her strong feelings about equal opportunities for all often come through in her stories. She and Caroline Binch first introduced Grace in *Amazing Grace*.
The illustrator	Caroline Binch's style is almost photographic but there is a great sense of character and movement in the pictures. She uses colour boldly. For her own book, *Gregory Cool*, she created both the written text and the illustrations.
Activities	• Section A will help pupils track the growth of the main character's changing perceptions;
• Section B will encourage pupils to complete textual gaps;
• Section C will help pupils verbally interpret the illustrations.
Assessment	The ability to:
• identify (through a sequencing activity) Grace's emotional growth;
• make explicit the gaps in the text, where information is given indirectly;
• read the illustrations and verbalise the details shown.
Related reading	The first story about Grace was *Amazing Grace*. Others include: *A Balloon for Grandad* by Nigel Gray and Jane Ray; *The Patchwork Quilt* by Valerie Flournoy and Jerry Pinkney; *Jazeera's Journey* by Lisa Bruce; *Granpa Chatterji* by Jamila Gavin and *Comfort Herself* by Geraldine Kaye.

3 Grace & Family

by Mary Hoffman
Illustrated by Caroline Binch

A 1 Grace's feelings about families develop throughout the book. Put the following comments into a new order which shows Grace's changing feelings. You'll need to know the book well and to skim and scan.

a) I'm not going to let this stepmother feed me or take me to the forest or anything!
b) I've forgotten what a real father is like.
c) I'm going to make up a story about a family like mine.
d) The mother in this family is not right. She's not my mother.
e) I wonder will my father still love me?
f) I like hearing the story about how much my father loves me.
g) They don't need me. They've already got a girl.
h) All proper families have a mother, a father, a boy, a girl, a dog and a cat.
i) I love my African family.
j) Families (like stories) are what you make them.
k) I can't manage two families.
l) I remember him!
m) I want a father who brings me roses.
n) I haven't got a father.
o) I won't upset my new brother and sister by telling them stories about wicked stepmothers.

B 2 In the book, there are many occasions on which the characters write, think or tell something but we, the readers, only hear about it indirectly or we have to guess it. The occasions are:

- the letter Grace's father writes, enclosing two air tickets;
- the story Grace's father tells her in return for Grace's promise that she will be nice to Jatou;
- the bedtime stories that Grace tells Neneh and Bakary;
- the telephone conversation which Grace has with her Ma in England;
- the wish that Grace makes at the crocodile holy place;
- the story Grace makes up about her new, bigger family.

Choose one of these and try to imagine what was written, told or thought. Then write it up and see if others think it fits the book.

C 3 Caroline Binch, the illustrator, is well known for her realistic pictures of people's facial expressions and clothes. *Either:* from the illustrations, write a list of words that describe the feelings that we see in Grace's face.

Or: from the illustrations make a list of the clothes that Grace and her Nana bring with them and buy in Africa. Describe them well enough for your classmates to identify the actual illustrations.

CRACKING GOOD BOOKS © *Judith Graham* 1997

4
The Shape-Changer

by Julian Atterton

Illustrated by Nigel Murray

First published by Julia MacRae, 1985; in paperback by Walker Books, 1989
ISBN 0-7445-1385-5

Genre	Historical, fantasy, mystery, magical, love story
Narrative voice	Third person narrative focused on Kari
Theme	The power of hate overturned by the power of love
Characters	The Viking settlers, Olaf and Halla; their son Kari; Colman, an Irishman and his daughter Ellen; the lame Norseman Grim; Harald, the Priest-Chieftain; Hild, the Deep-Minded; Catha and her various 'shape-changes'
Setting	The North York Moors
Era	Over 1100 years ago, in the time of the Vikings
Language	**Figurative:** Some similes: Ellen 'her eyes were as green as oak leaves at midsummer and her hair was as brown as bracken in autumn'; metaphor: the valley 'curls' away; alliteration: the shape 'shimmers and shifts'
	Use of standard/dialect: Standard throughout
	Use of direct speech: A balance of dialogue and narration
	Other: The simplicity and concreteness of the language matches the nature of the tale and the times. There is the occasional archaic word order, for example 'Fool are you to think you can overcome my magic' and some technical terms, mostly guessable from context, for example 'shieling', 'intake', 'garth'.
Story structure	**Opening:** Vikings Olaf, Holla and Kari arrive from Scandinavia and settle in the valley they name Westerdale. They prosper and are highly respected.
	Inciting moment: Kari goes in search of his sheep after a storm but finds them dead in a distant valley. Ellen approaches but when he asks for shelter she reveals that her father will prove unwelcoming as a curse lies on them.
	Development: Kari promises to break the spell but discovers that the cause of their misfortune is a cruel, shape-changing creature who persecutes them. He asks advice of his father, the Priest-Chieftain, and eventually from Hild who tests his worthiness with a dry stone-walling task. Hild passes on essential advice but the task becomes urgent as Ellen is wasting away on her sickbed. Kari learns of Colman's past from him and, armed with three arrows cut from a rowan tree, gives chase to the Shape-Changer in its several disguises.
	Denouement: The Shape-Changer is eventually revealed as Colman's first love, Catha. The final magic brings everyone back to health and youth.
	Ending: Ellen and Kari marry and are known as the Luck Bringers.
The author	Julian Atterton is a writer of historical fiction (see below) and has written two books about Robin Hood for younger readers. He lives in North Yorkshire and can see the moors from his attic study.
The illustrator	Nigel Murray is Head of Art at a London comprehensive and has illustrated *Heidi*.
Activities	The activities aim to: • enter and recreate story and characters' thoughts; • to show creative response.
Assessment	The ability to: • retell the story, retaining key points; • ask and answer questions in role; • read between the lines, expressing characters' unspoken thoughts; • create a further story, showing response to setting and style.
Related reading	*The Stone Book Quartet* by Alan Garner; *Vikings' Dawn* by Henry Treece; *The Fire of the Kings* and *The Last Harper* by Julian Atterton; *Dawn Wind* by Rosemary Sutcliffe; titles about North Yorkshire, for example *The Flither Pickers* by Theresa Tomlinson

4 The Shape-Changer

by Julian Atterton

Illustrated by Nigel Murray

Page references are to the Walker Books 1989 paperback edition.

A 1. The story of *The Shape-Changer* would work very well as a *told* story. This doesn't mean you have to learn it off by heart though you may find yourself using expressions from the book. If you can divide the story into six sections (according to the six chapters), each group in the class could prepare a telling of their section. It often helps to draw pictures of the key moments or to 'walk' the scenes through. You won't be able to tell everything so as a group you must decide what must be kept in. For instance, in the first chapter, it is important that you keep the storm in as this starts off the whole drama of the lost sheep and the meeting with Ellen. When you are ready, do not have any of your preparation notes near you, otherwise you'll be tempted to read them and your fluency will be lost.

2. In a group, decide that one (or more) of you is going to be in the 'hot-seat' as the Shape-Changer but now the spell is broken so it is as Catha that she will answer questions from the rest of the group. Ask Catha about the past and about what she regrets; ask her about the future and what she hopes for. Ask her about all the shapes she has turned into and what that was like.

3. Although there is lots of dialogue in the book, there are also occasions when the characters are lost in their own thoughts and we as readers have to imagine what they are thinking. Look back at the following parts of the book and choose one of these moments to try to write down the thoughts of the character. If it is possible, you could tape-record this 'interior monologue'.

   a) Kari's thoughts as he walks back with Ellen to her farmhouse (pages 13–14).

   b) Kari's thoughts as he is building the sheepfold (pages 27–29).

   c) Ellen's thoughts as she lies on her sickbed (page 33).

   d) Colman's thoughts as he sits alone after telling Kari his story (pages 34–36).

   e) Catha's thoughts when (in the form of a kitten) she overhears Colman's answers to Kari's questions about his love for her (pages 57–59).

B 4. Kari and Ellen marry and have five children and the author of the book says 'there are many stories worth telling about them'. Invent and write down one of those stories. Keep as close as you can to the feeling created in the book of the wildness and openness of the moors and, if you can, use some of the characters and places we already know.

CRACKING GOOD BOOKS © Judith Graham 1997

5 Storm

by Kevin Crossley-Holland
Illustrated by Alan Marks
First published by Heinemann, 1985
ISBN 0 434 93032 6
Winner of the Carnegie Medal, 1985

Genre	Short story, mystery story, ghost story. A mix of reality and fantasy
Narrative voice and devices	Third person, some flashback, some story within a story
Theme	Conquering personal fear for a greater cause. Rite of passage
Characters	Annie Carter, approximately nine years old; her elderly, infirm parents; Willa, her pregnant sister; a mysterious horseman
Setting	Isolated marshland and the village of Waterslain. Christmas holiday, wild storm, day and night
Era	Present day, with reference to legend from past
Language	Figurative: Rich in metaphor: 'sheets of rain'; simile: feeling 'stiff as a whingeing hinge'; personification: of fear, of the wind, of the storm, the moon, the rain
	Use of standard/dialect: Standard throughout
	Use of direct speech: Lots, and some interior monologue
	Other: Child sings words of song. Some of the patterning, repetition, alliteration, reversed word order and images give the story a poetic feel
Story structure	Opening: Scene set, Annie and her family and their significant features introduced, including Annie's knowledge of the fens and her fear of the ford. Her parents' infirmity stressed. Pregnant Willa comes to stay.
	Inciting moment: Willa goes into labour at the height of a storm. The phone is found to be out of order.
	Development: Annie volunteers to go for the doctor. A mysterious horseman arrives to take her behind him on his horse.
	Denouement: They successfully arrive at the doctor's.
	Ending: The horseman's identity is revealed.
The author	Kevin Crossley-Holland lives in East Anglia and is known for his editing of myths and legends and for his rewriting of traditional tales. He has recently worked again with Alan Marks on a retelling of *The Green Children*.
The illustrator	Alan Marks is the illustrator of *Thomas and the Tinners* (see page 34 of *Cracking Good Books*) and has illustrated Mother Goose rhymes and *David Copperfield*.
Activities	• Section A encourages the close inspection of the text to identify the author-laid clues so that predictions (made on page 15 of *Storm*) have a chance of being narratively likely. The clues are laid in several areas: the setting of the isolated cottage, the characters' chief traits and relationships, the story of the horseman, the existence of the telephone, and the foul weather. Acceptable predictions rely upon knowing what to attend to and what to ignore. The activities should develop and confirm pupils' competence in this area.
	• Section B will help pupils start to evaluate a complete text. The evaluative comments are typical reactions from readers of this story. They provide a model for the pupils to write an evaluative comment of their own.
Assessment	The ability to: • base acceptable prediction on close reading of text; • offer evaluative comment.
Related reading	*Brave Irene* by William Steig; *Ghost Stories* by Susan Hill and Angela Barrett; *The Wedding Ghost* by Leon Garfield and Charles Keeping; *A Bag of Moonshine* by Alan Garner and P. J. Lynch

5 Storm

by Kevin
Crossley-Holland
Illustrated by
Alan Marks

A *Read to the end of page 15.*

1. Talk with your partner, group or teacher about what you think will happen next. If you are reading alone, jot down your prediction on paper.

    Activities 2–6 will help you sharpen your prediction.

2. Draw a simple family tree for the Carter family. Add their approximate ages and one word to describe each character.

3. Draw a map of where the Carters live. Indicate where the river Rush and the village of Waterslain are and use some of the detail from the book to show what the marshland looks like.

4. Fill in one event that happens on each of the following days.

    Day 1 (the day the story begins):

    Day 2:

    Days 3 and 4:

    Night of Day 4:

5. Can you find four details that show that this story is set in modern times?

6. Can you write down the names of the three people who have told Annie about the ghost?

7. Now look back at your prediction. Do you want to change it at all?

B *After reading the book*

8. Talk with others who have also finished the story. Share the parts you liked and those you thought would be different.

9. Here are some comments from readers made after they had finished *Storm*. Discuss them in a group or tick those you agree with.

    > 'I thought the story should have been longer. It seemed unfinished.'
    > 'I don't think you should have stories about going off with strangers. It gives the wrong message.'
    > 'I liked the way Annie swallowed her fear for her sister's sake. Her bravery made the story very gripping.'
    > 'I found the story predictable which made it not so good.'
    > 'I found the story predictable but I enjoyed it.'
    > 'The ghost shouldn't have told Annie who he was. That should have been left to us to work out.'
    > 'I liked the way the title could have been about the weather or the ghostly horseman or the new-born baby.'

10. Now write a sentence or two to sum up your opinion of the story.

CRACKING GOOD BOOKS © *Judith Graham* 1997

6
Harry the Poisonous Centipede

by Lynne Reid Banks
Illustrated by Tony Ross
First published by Collins Children's Books, 1996
ISBN 0 00 675197 0

Genre	Humorous parable, fantasy
Narrative voice and devices	Mainly a third person narrative but with some comments and appeals made directly to the reader by the author
Theme	Growing up, forays into the big wide world
Characters	Harry, his mother Belinda, his friend George – all poisonous centipedes; a Hoo-Min (human)
Setting	Under and over ground in the tropics
Era	Present day
Language	Figurative: Some idioms rewritten to reflect the centipedes' world: 'don't count your ants' eggs before they are hatched'. Mostly straightforward

Use of standard/dialect: A few over-generalisations: 'most dangerousest'

Use of direct speech: More recounting than dialogue

Other: Colloquial tone especially in opening chapters; invention in terms used to describe the world from the centipedes' point of view: 'daytime = the brightness', 'smoke = white-choke'. Highlighting of unusual word: '*incorrigible*' |
| **Story structure** | Opening: The author introduces us to Harry and his mother Belinda and to their underground world. Belinda is a loving mother and she warns Harry about the dangers in 'the big, open, no-top world' above their heads. She shows him a particularly dangerous spot, the 'Up-Pipe' (a human's shower pipe).

Inciting moment and developments: Harry, occasionally goaded on by his friend George (a 'bad influence' according to Belinda), starts to explore forbidden places and hair-raising adventures follow. He is terrified and endangered but always ready for more.

Denouement: Belinda ultimately has to rescue the young centipedes from the world of the Hoo-Mins but they in turn save her life. She tells the story of the fate that befell Harry's father.

Ending: Harry and George realise the difference between recklessness and bravery (but secretly enjoy musing on possible adventures). |
| **The author** | Perhaps most famous for *The Indian in the Cupboard*, Lynne Reid Banks is the author of several titles for younger and older children. |
| **The illustrator** | Tony Ross is the author and illustrator of many popular picture books such as *Michael* and *I want my potty!* He is also a line illustrator and cover artist. |
| **Activities** | • Section A will help pupils select information from the text;
• Section B will help pupils to track the separate adventures that make up the plot;
• Section C will help pupils to notice one aspect of the author's use of language and to create words of their own on the same basis;
• Section D encourages pupils to take on some of the human relevance and emotional depths of the story through the creation of an extra episode. |
| **Assessment** | The ability to:
• identify relevant factual information;
• track the events of the plot;
• use language in specific ways, modelled on the author's use;
• see how character, emotion and plot are woven together. |
| **Related reading** | *The Hodgeheg* by Dick King-Smith; *Dinner at Alberta's* by Russell Hoban; *Willie the Squowse* by Ted Allen; *The Short Voyage of Albert Ross* by Jan Mark |

6
Harry the Poisonous Centipede

by Lynne Reid Banks

Illustrated by
Tony Ross

A *Read or re-read the first two chapters*

1 Fill in the following 'information file' on Harry.
   Species:
   Country where found:
   Habitat:
   Appearance and size:
   Health/survival needs:
   Food:
   How food caught:
   Main predator/enemy:
   Language and example of language:

B 2 Look at the map of Harry's World at the start of the book. Make a version of this map for yourself, perhaps a little larger. As you read, add more detail and notes around the edge to describe and locate the various adventures that happened to Harry or to Harry and George together. By the end of the book, you should have about six different stories surrounding the map.

C 3 The author of the book has obviously enjoyed herself making up names that the centipedes have for the creatures which they eat or which eat them. What creatures do you think are: belly-crawlers, flying-swoopers, belly-wrigglers, creepy-crawlers, furry biters, hairy-biters?

You can see that the author takes two aspects of the creature (perhaps how it moves and what it looks like) and then puts them together with a hyphen. The part after the hyphen is always a noun; the part before the hyphen can be another noun or an adjective.

Now make up some names for the following, remembering to use characteristics of the creature as they would appear to a centipede:

   mosquito   snail
   slug   hedgehog
   monkey   elephant

D 4 On the surface, this book is about centipedes but underneath it is about children growing up everywhere. They explore, they disobey, they egg each other on, they are excited, terrified and endangered. The author also shows us feelings of guilt, remorse, anxiety, love, loyalty, forgiveness, imagination and determination. Your task is to create another adventure for Harry (with or without George) in which some of these feelings are shown. It will be helpful if you discuss your ideas with a writing partner, perhaps sharing personal experiences on which you can base a centipede adventure!

CRACKING GOOD BOOKS © *Judith Graham 1997*

7 'The chicken gave it to me'

by Anne Fine
Illustrated by Philippe Dupasquier
First published by Methuen Children's Books, 1992; in paperback by Mammoth, 1993
ISBN 0 7497 1477 8
Winner of the Carnegie Medal

Genre	Comic, satirical novel with serious undertones
Narrative voice	Chapters alternate between a third person narrative and the first person narrative of the chicken's story.
Theme	Humane treatment of living things, altruism
Characters	Andrew and Gemma (probably about 8 or 9 years old); the chicken; school mates including Vinit the vegetarian; various caged humans; various little green men, including a TV chat show host and a radio voice
Setting	Story 1: school classroom and dining hall, the walk home. Story 2: the farm sheds, the spacecraft, the green planet and its TV studios
Era	Present day
Language	Figurative: The chicken uses alliteration: 'Fortune favours the feathery', and puns: 'Call me chicken no longer'.
	Use of standard/dialect: Standard throughout. Some Americanisms
	Use of direct speech: Lots. Chicken's thoughts are delivered as talk.
	Other: Colloquial, melodramatic, witty, dry style of chicken compares with Gemma and Andrew's thoughtful and passionate conversations. TV chat show host has soft 'honey' tones. Chicken gets message across in rhyming couplets. Interesting use of italics for various different purposes.
Story structure	Opening: Andrew convinces Gemma that the scratchily written book that he shows her was given to him by a chicken. They start to read.
	Inciting moment: Within the chicken's story, the release of the chickens by the green men and the subsequent caging of humans sets the chicken on her missionary course.
	Development: She stows away on the spacecraft and, through TV appearances on the green planet, the chicken has a profound effect on attitudes.
	Denouement: The chicken returns to earth, contented with her efforts.
	Ending: During their reading of the chicken's story, the children have reflected on all the issues to do with inhumane farming methods.
The author	Anne Fine lives in Barnard Castle and is the author of over two dozen humorous and serious books for older and younger readers. She has received all the major awards for children's fiction.
The illustrator	Philippe Dupasquier is a prolific illustrator of children's books and has created his own picture books such as *Going West*.
Activities	• Section A enables the pupil to draw evidence about character from the first-person narrative in the book. The obituary given will provide pupils with a useful vocabulary.
	• Section B helps pupils gather information from narrative text and to present it in an argued letter, in a sequenced and logical way. Both activities introduce new genres.
Assessment	The ability to: • find evidence to support a character study; • select, respond to and re-present the serious ethical questions raised.
Related reading	Dick King-Smith's books frequently champion animal rights as do *Meet the Greens* by Sue Limb and *Attila the Hen* by Paddy Hounter. Other Anne Fine books, for example *Bill's New Frock* and *The Angel of Nitshill Road*, deal with serious issues within a humorous narrative. Both of these books exist as playscripts.

7 'The chicken gave it to me'

by Anne Fine
Illustrated by
Philippe Dupasquier

A 1. Imagine that the chicken (now called Mission Chicken) lived her full life span and that she died when Gemma and Andrew were 17 or 18. They wrote this obituary of her.

> Mission Chicken 1992–1999
>
> The Mission Chicken, as she came to be called after her campaign to prevent cruelty on farms, has died aged 7 years. She was found resting in peace on her first and only book, *The Tale of Harrowing Farm*. This was the book that was so successful at alerting humans to the horrors of battery farms.
>
> From her book, we learn a great deal about Mission Chicken and her early life. She was a brave, positive and compassionate animal. Her determination was evident in all she did as was her dignity and stoicism. She became a great TV character and argued her points powerfully, persuading millions of the rightness of her cause. She had a wonderful way of speaking, often piling up the adjectives, speaking in rhyme, cracking dry jokes and exaggerating dramatically. She loved her food and indeed was generally a chicken who enjoyed all experiences. She endeared herself to everybody with her modesty. She had a way of laughing at herself which was charming. We are sure she died a proud and contented hen after a full life in the open air.

Your task is to find evidence in the book to show what Gemma and Andrew were basing their comments on in this description of the chicken's character.

B 2. Write a letter to the Minister of Agriculture, stating what you think the rights of hens are. Use points made in the book by Gemma and Andrew as well as what the green men say when they first see the battery hens and of course what the chicken herself says. You can also make use of the 'lies' in the *On the Farm* book that Andrew and Gemma look at.

Make additional points of your own if you feel it will help your letter sound even more persuasive.

8
Harriet's Hare

by Dick King-Smith
Illustrated by Valerie Littlewood
First published by Doubleday, 1994; in paperback by Corgi Yearling, 1996
ISBN 0 440 86340 6
Winner of the Children's Book Award, 1995

Genre	Magic realism
Narrative voice	Third person, some interior thoughts of father and Harriet
Theme	Loneliness transformed through friendliness, keeping promises, good nature, luck – and more than a little magic. Match-making and mating practices
Characters	Harriet, aged about 8; her widowed father, John Butler; Mrs Wisker, who helps in their house; Jessica, a divorcee and newcomer to the village; a visitor from the planet Pars, who mostly takes the form of a hare and is named Wiz by Harriet.
Setting	Longhanger Farm in Wiltshire during the summer holidays
Era	Present day
Language	Figurative: Very little: the farmhouse 'tucked' into the side of a hill, a field looking 'like a square gold blanket'; puns, including one on 'occidentalis/accidentalis'
	Use of standard/dialect: Mrs Wisker speaks in the Wiltshire dialect: 'he hadn't no more sense than an old sheep'
	Use of direct speech: The greater part of the book is in dialogue.
	Other: Clever use of complex words in context: omnilingual. Language very accessible with occasional irony and understatement
Story structure	Opening: Harriet is woken at dawn by a loud swishing noise.
	Inciting moment: She discovers a corn circle in the field and, to her surprise, a talking hare approaches her. He reveals that he is a visitor from the planet Pars and that he has chosen to visit Earth in the form of a hare. Harriet names the hare Wiz and endears herself to him because she is motherless, fond of animals generally and concerned for Wiz's safety in particular. She keeps her hare a secret as requested.
	Development: The hare pursues two distinct plans: the first is to bring Jessica, a newcomer to the village, and Harriet's father together; the second, conducted more discreetly, is to find a mate for himself. Harriet is unaware of Wiz's schemes and is more concerned with his imminent return to Pars at the coming full moon.
	Denouement: Both Wiz's projects bear fruit.
	Ending: Wiz departs and Harriet at last realises his role in her family's new-found happiness. She has Wiz's three leverets and long life to look forward to.
The author	Dick King-Smith has been both a farmer and a teacher and his affection for both animals and children is apparent in his many books. His first book *The Fox Busters* was published in 1978 and he is probably best known for *The Sheep-Pig* which has been made into the film, *Babe*.
The illustrator	Valerie Littlewood is a freelance children's book illustrator.
Activities	The activities aim to: • develop a reflective awareness of how the text is constructed, particularly in terms of traditional story shape but also in terms of how the author drops clues which attentive readers pick up; • encourage wider reading.
Assessment	The ability to: • read aloud; • read closely and to pick up contextual clues; • analyse an author's narrative techniques (particularly openings).
Related reading	Many of Dick King-Smith's titles are cheerful animal fantasies. They include *Saddlebottom* and *Martin's Mice*.

8
Harriet's Hare

by Dick King-Smith

Illustrated by Valerie Littlewood

Page references are to the Corgi Yearling 1996 paperback edition.

A 1 If you are working in a group, take one of the following passages each and prepare a reading-aloud of the section.

   a) Page 10 ('As she stood there now…') to page 13 ('We Partians have the ability to change.')

   b) Page 16 ('"Tell me a bit about yourself…"') to page 19 ('"Wiz," she said.')

   c) Page 21('"There's a corn circle, Dad!"') to page 24 ('"Not long now," he said.')

   d) Page 26 ('Just then she saw…') to page 31 ('"I want to get back to Pars in one piece."')

2 In these four passages, all the reasons behind Wiz's plans to improve Harriet's life are hidden. Can you find them? You should try to answer this question: 'Why does Wiz decide to help Harriet?'

B *Either:*

3a Were you surprised when Wiz showed Harriet his daughters? If you look back through the book, there are enough hints that he was having a very enjoyable private life with the female hare he has met. Harriet doesn't pick up the hints but *we* do and that adds to the enjoyment of the book.

Find and write down three or four clues that the author drops about Wiz's private life which we can understand when we look back. You will find them in Chapters 3, 4, 8 and 9.

Or:

3b Were you surprised when Harriet's father and Jessica tell Harriet that they are going to be married? If you look back through the book, there are enough hints that this was going to happen and that this is what Wiz was plotting. Harriet doesn't pick up the hints but *we* do and that adds to the enjoyment of the book.

Find and write down three or four clues that the author drops about Harriet's father and Jessica which we can understand when we look back. You will find them in Chapters 2, 3, 5, 6, 7, 8, 9 and 10.

C 4 *Harriet's Hare* has a very dramatic opening. What could be more action-packed and exciting than being woken at five in the morning by what turns out to be a spacecraft landing? The information about the characters and the time and place are very cleverly slotted in later in the chapter. Does Dick King-Smith always do this in his books? Collect as many of his titles together as you can and research:

   a) the ways in which he starts his stories dramatically;

   b) the ways in which he gives his readers other information.

Share your findings by reading and reporting back to your group.

9 The Little Riders

by Margaretha Shemin
Illustrated by Peter Spier
First published by Coward, McCann and Geoghegan, USA, 1963; Julia MacRae, 1988; in paperback by Walker Books, 1990
ISBN 0 7445 1751 6

Genre	War-time adventure story, child heroine. Credible if not exactly true
Narrative voice	Third person, linear narrative
Theme	Courage, and the human face of the 'enemy'
Characters	Eleven year old Johanna; her grandparents; Captain Braun; her father; the twelve mechanical horsemen: the Little Riders
Setting	Various rooms in Johanna's grandparents' home in a mediaeval town (Alkmaar) north of Amsterdam, Holland; the church opposite. Late summer moving into a bitter winter
Era	The last year of World War II
Language	Figurative: Very little
	Use of standard/dialect: Standard throughout
	Use of direct speech: A balance of description and dialogue
	Other: Straightforward, direct language. A few technical war terms
Story structure	Opening: Johanna, separated from her American parents, is living with her grandparents in occupied Holland. Her attic bedroom window overlooks the church tower with its twelve iron horsemen which emerge on the hour. The attic has a hidden cupboard. The apologetic, flute-playing Captain Braun requisitions Johanna's room. Johanna has to sleep in her grandfather's den.
	Inciting moment: An order arrives that the Little Riders must be dismantled for melting down for armaments.
	Development: Grandparents and Johanna remove the figures from the church and hide them in the den. A plan to further remove the Little Riders is thwarted and angry soldiers take Joanna's grandparents away for questioning. Joanna is left alone before the soldiers return to search the house. Johanna is discovered by the returning Captain Braun while attempting to hide figures in 'his' cupboard. He admires the figures and helps Johanna hide them.
	Denouement: The figures are not found and Captain Braun reveals nothing.
	Ending: The war ends, the occupying forces leave, Joanna's father is amongst the liberating troops. Captain Braun leaves Johanna his flute.
The author	The author was born in Alkmaar, the town of the story. The Little Riders which come out from the tower as the clock strikes are now a tourist attraction.
The illustrator	Also from Holland, Peter Spier is well known for his line and colour work to traditional rhymes.
Activities	• Section A encourages the extracting of information from the text and the tracking of the many clues laid by the author about Captain Braun's true nature;
	• Section B will help pupils perceive the structure of the book through recall and selection of the key dramatic moments of the text.
Assessment	The ability to:
	• extract information from the text and to perceive how an author builds up the portrait of a character;
	• re-call and re-tell the story through focus on key events.
Related reading	*The Borrowed House* and *The Winged Watchman* by Hilda van Stockum, *The Upstairs Room* by Johanna Reiss, *The Silver Sword* by Ian Serrailier, *When Hitler Stole Pink Rabbit* by Judith Kerr

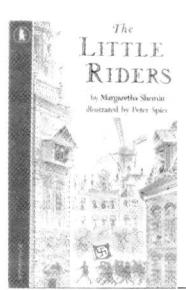

9 The Little Riders

by Margaretha Shemin

Illustrated by Peter Spier

Page references are to the Walker Books 1990 paperback edition.

A 1. The book gives a clear idea of what it was like to live in a country occupied by enemy troops during the second world war. Make a list of 10 details that the author mentions that help build up the feeling of life being different, frightening and less free. Here are two to start with:

a) Johanna can't return to America;

b) White bulletins appear on the street corners printed with the names of hostages and orders from the German commander.

2. The author drops many hints in the book that Captain Braun is a sensitive man and that he is not going to be an enemy of Johanna and her grandparents. Make a list of 10 clues that we are given that reveal Captain Braun to be a kind and thoughtful man. Here are two to start you off:

a) He rings the bell quietly;

b) He apologises to the grandparents for taking over Johanna's room.

B 3. You are probably familiar with the short pamphlets you can pick up when you go into a famous building or church. They usually tell you a bit about the history of the place and important things to look out for. Your task is to write a tourist brochure for the church in the town of the story (Alkmaar), describing the Little Riders and particularly telling the story of what happened to them during World War II. You may want to draw the Little Riders to decorate your pamphlet.

4. Captain Braun goes back to his family at the end of the war. Imagine that they ask him what has happened to his flute in its embroidered case. Write the story he tells them.

5. Re-read pages 45–52. Imagine you were asked to provide music for a film or radio play of this part of the story. Describe the type of music you would need to accompany the different events that happen.

6. Look through the book again at Peter Spier's illustrations. The publisher writes to him to say that they would like two more illustrations. Which moments will he choose to illustrate? Write his letter back to the publishers, explaining the reasons for his choice.

CRACKING GOOD BOOKS © *Judith Graham* 1997

10 Sir Gawain and the Green Knight

Retold by Selina Hastings
Illustrated by Juan Wijngaard
First published by Walker Books, 1981; in paperback by Walker Books, 1991
ISBN 0-7445-2005-3

Genre	Romantic legend/pseudo history
Narrative voice	Impersonal third person narrator
Theme	Honour and bravery put to the test
Characters	King Arthur, the Green Knight (alias Sir Bercilak), Sir Gawain, Sir Bercilak, Sir Bercilak's wife, Morgan le Fay (in disguise)
Setting	The court of King Arthur, the castle and Green Chapel of Sir Bercilak, the wild land of Britain in between. Bitter winter
Era	Late 14th century?
Language	Figurative: Little
	Use of standard/dialect: Standard throughout
	Use of direct speech: More narration than dialogue
	Other: The complex sentences, use of the subjunctive, use of present participles, reversed word order and rhythmic prose capture an authentic period feel. Some technical terms may be difficult, for example 'cuisses', 'greaves', 'pennants', 'damask'. Some expressions may be obscure though able to be guessed from context, for example 'faltered', 'brandishing', 'prowess', 'gallantry'.
Story structure	Opening: Christmas is being celebrated at the court of King Arthur.
	Inciting moment: The dramatic figure of the Green Knight enters. He throws out a challenge to the knights. Sir Gawain is eager to meet it and strikes off the Green Knight's head. The Green Knight calmly picks it up and leaves, reminding Sir Gawain to meet him as agreed in a year and a day.
	Development: Sir Gawain keeps his promise, arriving, after a hazardous journey, at the splendid castle of one Sir Bercilak. Another bargain is struck with the two men agreeing to exchange in the evening whatever each has won during the day. Sir Bercilak's wife attempts to seduce Sir Gawain but he conceals nothing from her husband but a protective girdle she has given him.
	Denouement: The Green Knight (alias Sir Bercilak) meets Sir Gawain at the Green Chapel as planned but, though he brings the axe down on his neck, he spares his life because of his courage and (near perfect) honesty.
	Ending: Sir Gawain returns to King Arthur's court amidst much rejoicing. Henceforth, all knights will wear a green girdle as a mark of honour.
The author	Selina Hastings is well known for her direct, clear, prose retellings of texts such as *The Canterbury Tales*.
The illustrator	Juan Wijngaard adapts his style to the text he is illustrating, reflecting old illuminated manuscripts in this book and in *Sir Gawain and the Loathly Lady* or 'old masters' as in *The Nativity*.
Activities	The activities aim to help pupils to: • evaluate the likeliness of events in the story; • look below the surface at the private feelings of the main character; • use illustration to form a picture of the period and to deepen significance.
Assessment	The ability to: • evaluate and respond imaginatively to a character's likely feelings; • consider the information content; • detect the symbolic depth of what pupils have read and noted in illustrations.
Related reading	Hastings and Wijngaard have produced a companion text, *Sir Gawain and the Loathly Lady* which won the Kate Greenaway award in 1985. Michael Morpurgo has retold the Arthurian legends in *Arthur, High King of Britain*, with illustrations by Michael Foreman.

10
Sir Gawain and the Green Knight

retold by **Selina Hastings**
Illustrated by
Juan Wijngaard

A 1 Sir Gawain and the whole of King Arthur's court were being put to the test in this story, by several people at Sir Bercilak's castle. Arthur almost certainly did live (in around 500 AD) and almost certainly was frequently challenged by people who were jealous of his power. However, some events in this story are unlikely to have happened. Make a chart with two headings: Possible and Impossible. Discuss the events of the story with your group and then put them under those two headings. You may need a third column for Unlikely.

B 2 Sir Gawain is the youngest of King Arthur's knights and, as he says, he has not yet had a chance to prove himself. Imagine he has been keeping a diary of his life since arriving at King Arthur's court. Write two entries, one *before* the Green Knight appears at King Arthur's court and one just *after*.

3 As the day approaches when Sir Gawain must go in search of the Green Chapel to keep his side of the bargain, his diary entries must reflect his mixed feelings. Write a typical entry.

4 Sir Gawain writes every evening about the events of the days spent at Sir Bercilak's castle. Write one or more of these entries.

5 Write the entry in Sir Gawain's diary when he is safely back home.

C 6 Look again at the illustrations in the book. They tell us about several aspects of life in the 14th century. Look particularly at:
- the armour and clothes of men and women of the court
- horse decoration
- the interiors and exteriors of castles
- the wild land of Britain.

Imagine you are contributing to an information book on this period. (This period is often called the Middle Ages.) Write an entry for the book under one of those four headings. Use the information in the illustrations and, if you wish, from the written text as well. You might also consult other useful texts.

7 One of the ways in which an illustrator can deepen the meaning of a book is by putting in details which are not mentioned in the written part of the story, leaving us to notice them or not. One such detail in this book is to do with the green girdle. Search the illustrations and then write about the significance of where the girdle is first pictured. You will need to have read through to the end of the book to make all the connections.

11 Celebration Song

by James Berry
Illustrated by Louise Brierley
First published by Hamish Hamilton, 1994; in paperback by Puffin Books, 1996
ISBN 0-1405-0716-7

Genre	Lyrical, illustrated poem
Narrative voice and devices	First person: Mary addressing the child Jesus. Flashback to the annunciation and nativity
Theme	Celebration
Characters	Mary and the infant Jesus
Setting	Seaside village – possibly Caribbean (in illustrations only)
Era	1 AD
Language	**Figurative:** Few conventional figures of speech
	Use of standard/dialect: Strictly standard though there seem to be echoes of a distinctive language
	Use of direct speech: Whole poem is a spoken tribute
	Other: Repeated sounds: 'day/say', 'light/lights', 'own/own', 'hurried/hurried', 'happen/happen', 'long/long'; unusual compound words: 'born-day', 'out-and-in dance'; intransitive verbs used transitively: 'Wind dances palm trees'; adjectives after nouns: 'the little baby found', 'little hands troublesome'. Ideas expressed compactly: 'All day music is in all of sky in my head'
Story structure	**Opening:** Mary speaks to Jesus of her pleasure in him and of the celebrational atmosphere everywhere. Creatures and plants behave unexpectedly in their joint jubilation. Mary tells her child the story of his annunciation and his birth. She plays with him and everybody celebrates, including fish and birds.
	Ending: Mary asks what the future will bring.
Illustrations	Extra story exists only in the illustrations which are strong, sculptured non-representational shapes, with symbolic changes in colour. We see Mary and Joseph and the whole community are black. They live beside the sea and the stable of Jesus' birth is on the seashore. Mary and Jesus are rowed across the sea to another island (or to the mainland) by a group of women musicians. Alone on the second island, they look out towards an uncertain territory of red rocks. We see that flags, pennants and banners fly to celebrate Jesus' first birthday and the whole text is handwritten on these flying banners.
The author	James Berry has received major awards for his poems (*When I Dance*) and his short stories (*The Thief in the Village*).
The illustrator	Louise Brierley has been an illustrator since 1986 and is known for both her tiny stick-like people and her strong sculptured forms. Both styles are evident in *The Orchard Book of Creation Stories* by M. Mayo.
Activities	• Section A helps pupils deepen their understanding of both written and illustrated text through the preparation of a reading;
	• Section B helps pupils add a verse to the poem, taking note of the range of the poem from fantasy to realism;
	• Section C encourages pupils to appraise the poem and its illustrations.
Assessment	The ability to:
	• convey understanding through a prepared reading;
	• pick out the fantastical and the realistic and write an extra verse;
	• evaluate the unusual in the book.
Related reading	Jan Pienkowski, Jane Ray and Brian Wildsmith have all produced picture books on biblical themes. Charles Causley has Christmas poems in *Bring in the Holly*.

11
Celebration Song

by James Berry
Illustrated by
Louise Brierley

A 1 Read and re-read the book. You may want to practise reading the verse aloud and getting used to its unusual rhythm and use of words. You may want to re-examine the illustrations and note the extra stories that they tell. Much of the book shows dance and music and you may want to try to capture that in a reading you give.

Turn to the pages that tell of Jesus' annunciation and birth. This part is like a flashback in a film. How do both author and illustrator indicate that this part is different?

Now turn to the last page in the book. Discuss the questions that Mary asks. Do you think the changed landscape is part of the answer to her questions?

Now present a reading to your class which conveys the changes at these parts of the poem.

B 2 Some parts of the poem are quite 'fantastical' such as the pages where 'Singing dogs bang tins'. Some are realistic and could be written about any baby, such as 'You tried to open my eyes yesterday when I dozed, not liking them shut.'

Try to write an extra verse to put into the poem, *either* describing more fantastic happenings *or* describing more typical games that one year old babies play or things that they do.

C 3 James Berry, the writer, and Louise Brierley, the illustrator, are both regarded as unusual in the way they approach their work. Discuss with your group what you have found in the book that is unusual. Then write a letter addressed to one of them (or to both of them), saying what you found to like in their approach to the traditional Christian story. You may also have some questions to which you would like answers.

You could post your letters to them at: Hamish Hamilton, 27, Wrights Lane, London, W8 5TZ. Both would be interested in your views and questions. You may even get a reply.

CRACKING GOOD BOOKS © *Judith Graham 1997*

12
The Battle of Bubble and Squeak

by Philippa Pearce
Illustrated by Alan Baker
First published by André Deutsch, 1978; in paperback by Puffin Books, 1980
ISBN 0 14 03.1183 1
Winner of the Whitbread Award, 1978

Genre	A realistic, intense family-and-animal story in eleven short chapters
Narrative voice and devices	Third person narrator but with some interior monologue giving access to the thoughts of several of the characters
Theme	Emotional adjustment within a family when two gerbils come to stay
Characters	Sid Parker, approximately eleven years old; his younger sisters, Peggy and Amy; his mother Alice and her second husband Bill Sparrow; some friends of the children – particularly Dawn Mudd; Mrs Pring and her cat Ginger; two gerbils, Bubble and Squeak
Setting	Family home on working-class estate on edge of village. One scene set at night in sinister local wood. Autumn to Christmas
Era	Present day
Language	Figurative: Metaphor and simile used sparingly but to great effect
	Use of standard/dialect: Standard throughout
	Use of direct speech: Lots, and interior monologue
	Other: Short, clean-cut sentences when the story requires it. Otherwise, more extended descriptive passages, for example when the gerbils' behaviour is observed
Story structure	Opening and inciting moment: There is a dramatic opening when Sid's gerbils reveal their presence in the middle of the night. Mother will not have them in the house.
	Development: Mrs Sparrow makes many attempts to dispose of the gerbils. All of these attempts backfire. Sid is extremely distressed. Stepfather Bill makes many reparative moves.
	Denouement: Amy's distress brings about understanding and a promise from her mother.
	Ending: Mother helps nurse Bubble back to health after being mauled by a cat and the family becomes united.
The author	Philippa Pearce lives near Cambridge, where she was born and where her first two novels for older readers are set, *Minnow on the Say* (1955) and *Tom's Midnight Garden* (1958, winner of the Carnegie Medal). She has written ten much-praised books for children, including four collections of short stories.
The illustrator	Alan Baker illustrates children's books, working mostly in pen and ink.
Activities	• Section A encourages looking back over the book to isolate and appreciate the story's main events. The framework given underlines the linked nature of the episodes and gives the pupils support in a task that requires their scanning of the whole book.
• Section B is designed to draw out an awareness of the differences in the characters and of how their conflicting needs and perspectives propel the plot. 2c pushes pupils to realise the deeper levels in the book, with the family's response to the gerbils perhaps representing their differing levels of acceptance of the loss of David Parker and the arrival of Bill Sparrow.
Assessment	The ability to:
• link events and episodes in the plot;
• see how characters and plot interact and reveal deeper significance.
Related reading	*A Dog So Small* by Philippa Pearce also concerns a child's longing for a pet amid parental opposition. Shirley Hughes has written and illustrated a lighter treatment of the theme in *Chips and Jessie*.

12 The Battle of Bubble and Squeak

by Philippa Pearce

Illustrated by Alan Baker

A 1 The 'battle' in this book swings backwards and forwards. Fill in the gaps in the following account of the plot.

The gerbils can't be given back to Jimmy Dean's cousin as he's in Australia *so…*

but Bill brings them back again. They gnaw holes in the red curtains so Mrs Sparrow puts a notice in the newsagent's and gives the gerbils to two little boys who call at the house *but… and…*

so Mrs Sparrow put the gerbils' cage out on dustbin day *but…*

so Mrs Sparrow promises not to send them away again. Sid is not sure that she can keep her promise *so…*

When the gerbils come back, they escape from the cage, and although they are successfully recaptured, Mrs Pring's cat has had a chance to meet them. The cat sneaks in through the back door whilst Bill has gone to fetch coal *and…*

Bubble is taken to the vet but Peggy can't hold Bubble's head right for the medicine *so…*

Bubble recovers and then Jimmy Dean's cousin turns up to claim the gerbils *but…*

and they all sit down happily to a meal of bubble-and-squeak.

B 2 You've looked at how the plot of the story develops in section A. But nothing would happen in that way if the characters in the story were different people. If Mrs Sparrow didn't hate the gerbils so much or if Bill Sparrow didn't want to be accepted by his wife and stepchildren or if the children didn't care so passionately about the gerbils there would be no story. With your group discuss the following questions about the characters:

a) Why does Mrs Sparrow hate the gerbils so much? Can you understand her behaviour at all? Can you forgive her?

b) Bill Sparrow is the new member of this family. He wants to be kind and sympathetic to the children and not upset his wife either. Mention some of the many ways in which he shows this.

c) Do you think that the three children's different ways of feeling about the gerbils are related to their different ages, maturity and gender? Do you think that each of them was and is differently affected by their father's death and their mother's re-marriage?

13 The Winter Sleepwalker

by Joan Aiken
Illustrated by Quentin Blake
First published by Jonathan Cape, 1994; in paperback by Random House, 1995
ISBN 0 09 949641 0

Genre	Short fantasy stories which often subvert the fairy tale genre
Narrative voice	Third person reliable narrator
Themes	Most of the stories involve the use and misuse of magic.
Characters	1) Prince, princess, king, coach driver, school teachers, bird. 2) Witch, shopkeepers (Bill, Trilla, Lootie). 3) Postman and daughter, queen, prince. 4) A sailor girl, King Neptune, their twin boys. 5) A granny, villagers, children and youths, monsters, a controller on Mars. 6) Mysterious horseman, villagers. 7) A miller and his daughter, a brown bear. 8) Little Saint Icarus, the Great Umpire in the Sky, a poet, a dog (Nameless) and Eve.
Settings	1) Imaginary mountainous kingdom, school, palace. 2) A village and its shops, witch's cottage and wood. 3) Palace, streets of Mercia, seashore. 4) Kingdom under the sea. 5) Norfolk village. 6) The village of Furious Hill atop jagged cliffs. 7) A watermill and hay barn on the edge of a mountain forest, a cave. 8) The heavens before and after the big bang, planet Earth.
Era	Most stories set in a timeless era though nearly all refer to modern gadgets (for example cameras, TV) and modern ideas/practices (e.g. playing football).
Language	**Figurative:** Rich in similes: 'rope… laid flat… like ribs of sand over the floor'; metaphor: 'baking a first class volcano'; personification: 'a deadly fear came sliding into his heart'; alliteration: 'drooped and dwindled, sighed and sagged, flickered and flopped'
	Use of standard/dialect: Standard, except in the speech of the Vickers' boys
	Use of direct speech: Every story has lively dialogue, often witty
	Other: Patterning, repetition and wild images coupled with a ruthless logic make for rich text. Various songs
Story outlines	1) Magic blue boots and a bird bring happiness to the palace. 2) Mrs Hatecraft's new broom doesn't bring her joy. 3) An accidental loss, a curse, a happy ending. 4) Marriage between a sailor girl and King Neptune sours. 5) The sons of the previous pairing save their village from monsters. 6) A mysterious horseman is treated shabbily by the villagers he's helped. 7) A wood-carving miller is cruelly but aptly punished for cutting down an oak tree. 8) Little Saint Icarus, goalkeeper to the galaxy, blows a fuse in the universe and is punished by the 'umpire'.
The author	Born in 1924, Joan Aiken lives in New York and Sussex. *Wolves of Willoughby Chase* was her first children's book and she followed that fantasy–historical novel with many others. Her short stories are collected in such volumes as *The Kingdom under the Sea*, *A Necklace of Raindrops* and *Past Eight O'Clock*.
The illustrator	Quentin Blake is a prolific and popular illustrator who has contributed his fluid illustrations to poetry, classic and modern novels and to his own and others' picture books.
Activities	• Section A will help pupils appreciate the raw ingredients of the Aiken stories. There is an opportunity to construct a story of one's own, using the grid to help planning. • Section B will help pupils draw back and evaluate the stories. It allows for a more sophisticated appraisal, assessing features of John Aiken's style.
Assessment	The ability to: • close read the text and extract information; • construct a story of one's own, using Aiken's structuring characteristics; • offer evaluative comment and appreciate stylistic features.
Related reading	Other stories by Joan Aiken (see above).

13 The Winter Sleepwalker

by Joan Aiken
Illustrated by Quentin Blake

A 1. Copy the grid below. As you read the stories, discuss them and fill in the columns. The first story has been done for you.

Story	Opening or main event	Magic object	Magic person or animal	Sad parts	Funny/ up-to-date parts	Ending H = happy S = sad O = open
Over the Cloudy Mountain	the queen disappears	the blue shoes	queen, blue bird, head-mistress	queen's death (?) king's and prince's grief	Teb not wanting to wear a girl's shoe, camera, school	the bird unravels the rope and they find the mother's note (O)
Blazing Shadows						
Melusina						
A Basket of Water						
The Liquorice Tree						
Furious Hill						
The Winter Sleepwalker						
Catch a Falling World						

B Here are some comments from readers which they made after finishing all the stories. Discuss them in a group.

'The story I liked best was "Melusina" because it was funny. The granny said about Melusina turning into a snake on Sundays, "It must be something on your father's side of the family. No one in *my* family *ever* turned into a pink snake." I liked the way the mum was off on a space mission and the granny was having her hearing aid fixed.'

'The story I didn't like was "Blazing Shadows" because I wanted the dog to be not a holly bush any more. Trilla should have used the broom to turn him back into a dog. Maybe she didn't see the witch do that so she didn't know.'

'The story I found hardest to understand was "Furious Hill" because I don't know what the traveller kept asking about. And you don't know what happens to the houses. I think they're going to go up in flames. It's quite spooky.'

'The saddest story was "The Winter Sleepwalker". I keep thinking about the wooden girl and the wooden bear in the cave. I think that's the only way they could really get married so it's not really sad.'

2. Now write about the story you liked most (or least). You could also write about Joan Aiken's way of writing stories.

14 The Highwayman

by Alfred Noyes
Illustrated by Charles Keeping
First written in 1913. First published by Oxford University Press, 1981; in paperback by Oxford University Press, 1983
ISBN 0 19 272133 X
Winner of the Kate Greenaway Medal, 1982

Genre	Dramatic, narrative poem, picture book
Narrative voice	Third person, impersonal narrator
Theme	Romantic love, jealousy, self-sacrifice
Characters	The Highwayman; Bess, the landlord's daughter; Tim, the ostler; red-coats
Setting	A rural inn, its yard, Bess' room, the view from her window over the road
Era	First half of the 18th century (in the time of King George II)
Language	Figurative: Similes: hair like 'mouldy hay', 'dumb as a dog', 'burnt like a brand'; metaphors: the wind 'a torrent of darkness', the moon 'a ghostly galleon'; the road 'a ribbon of moonlight' and 'a gypsy's ribbon', hair 'a cascade of perfume'; alliteration: 'clattered and clashed'; onomatopoeia: 'tlot-tlot'
	Use of standard/dialect: Standard throughout
	Use of direct speech: A mixture
	Other: Reversed word order: 'blood-red were his spurs'; some archaisms: 'thee', 'press', 'pressgang', 'scarce', 'scarcely'
Verse features	Rhyme scheme (AABCCB) sustained throughout all 17 verses. The only half-rhymes are 'blood/good', 'blood/stood', 'again/refrain' and 'hear/there'. Lines are long with varying metre. The CC rhymes are always repetitions and are key words of the narrative: 'riding', 'daughter', 'moonlight', 'marching', 'window'.
Story structure	**Opening:** The Highwayman rides at night to the inn to see Bess.
	Inciting moment: Tim, the ostler, himself in love with Bess, lurks in the shadows and overhears the Highwayman's declaration of love and his plans to return.
	Development: Bess waits but, in the evening, King George's red-coats arrive. They bind and gag Bess. With her, they wait all day in view of the road down which the Highwayman will come. Unseen by the red-coats, Bess works her hand around to the trigger of the musket bound to her.
	Denouement: The Highwayman eventually comes as arranged but Bess releases the trigger and kills herself as a warning to him. The Highwayman is saved but when he learns of Bess' self-sacrifice, he returns and is himself killed.
	Ending: Legend has it that the lovers still meet on moonlit nights.
The author	Alfred Noyes, 1880–1958, born in Wolverhampton. He wrote in several genres but *The Highwayman* is now the only work well known.
The illustrator	Charles Keeping, 1920–1988, was born in Lambeth, South London and is well known as a line illustrator of fiction and as a full-colour picture book creator. His artwork is always original, evocative and unsentimental. Keeping countered the criticism that his illustrations for *The Highwayman* were too violent by saying he was bringing out the implicit violence in the poem.
Activities	• Section A helps pupils to focus on content, drama and verse aspects; • Section B examines the contribution and power of the illustrations; • Section C encourages the filling-in of the textual gaps and the appreciation of motive in a minor character.
Assessment	The ability to: • prepare and deliver a reading, sensitive to the poem's content and metre; • respond to illustrative detail and power; • make inferences and make the implicit explicit.
Related reading	Charles Keeping has also illustrated, in similar style, Tennyson's poem *The Lady of Shalott*. A poem with a similar theme is the anonymous *The Hangman's Tree*.

14 The Highwayman

by Alfred Noyes
Illustrated by Charles Keeping

A 1 In a group, prepare a dramatic reading of this poem. Decide where you will have a single reader and where you will read together. Decide how you will deal with dialogue and inner thoughts. Will sound effects (for example horses' hoofs or redcoats marching or the musket shot) add to your presentation?

It will help you with your reading if you get the stress or 'beat' of each line sorted out. One way of doing this is to put a short line over each syllable to be stressed,

> The wínd was a tórrent of dárkness amóng the gústy trées,
> The móon was a ghóstly gálleon tóssed upon clóudy séas.

Notice that the stress will not be in the same place for each verse and that although many of the lines have fifteen syllables, not all of them do:

> And dark in the dark old inn-yard a stable-wicket creaked
> Where Tim the ostler listened. His face was white and peaked.

B 2 Many readers find Charles Keeping's illustrations add a great deal to Alfred Noyes' words. Under each of the following headings, add further details to the examples given for you.

Period detail:
The Highwayman's clothes, for example his cocked hat

Atmosphere and tension:
The bare trees, the empty road

Symbolic power:
The cut-out hearts in the wooden shutters

Character detail:
The ostler's mad eyes

Helping with meaning:
The word 'priming' is explained.

Emotions:
Horror in the face of the Highwayman when he hears of Bess' death

C 3 Tim, the ostler, is a critically important person in the story. We do not see what he does but we can deduce it. We can 'read between the lines'. After you have read the poem and know it well, choose someone (or it can be more than one of you) in your group to be in the 'hot' seat, in role as the ostler. The rest of you should ask 'Tim' about the deaths of Bess and the Highwayman and about his motivation for doing what he did. Ask him whether he expected Bess to do what she did. Ask him if he feels guilty. Ask him what Bess' father thinks of him.

15 Princess Jazz and the Angels

by Rachel Anderson
First published by Heinemann, 1994; in paperback by Mammoth, 1995
ISBN 0 7497 2391 2

Genre	Realistic novel
Narrative voice	Third person plus main character interiorising
Theme	The discovery of identity
Characters	Ten year old Jaswinder (Jazz), daughter of Bridie O'Hare and her late husband, Rajinder Singh; Miss MacFadyen (social worker); foster parents; cousin Harjit and Grandmother (Oldest Auntiji) in the punjab; Dr Elspeth
Settings	Glasgow tenement flat, suburban house outside Glasgow, airports and aeroplane, rural Punjabi home, hospital, Temple of Amritsar
Era	Present day
Language	**Figurative:** Not a great deal but language is always lively, even gutsy
	Use of standard/dialect: Standard with some vivid Glasgow, Irish and Indian dialect, vocabulary and idiom
	Use of direct speech: Lots, and direct access to Jazz' thoughts
	Other: Complex emotions and thoughts expressed accessibly
Story structure	**Opening and inciting moment:** Jazz awakes to find her mother missing. She signs for a small parcel from the postman and then phones 999 from a callbox.
	Development: Jazz is put into care but the package contains a ticket to the Punjab so she flies out to meet her dead father's family. Jazz's confusion is evident as she behaves more and more unpleasantly until she finally insults her Grandmother and runs away to avoid a beating. She is found but not before she has eaten some rotten food. She falls seriously ill and is hospitalised.
	Denouement: Through the robust care of Dr Elspeth and the tender care of her relatives, Jazz recovers her health and gains an understanding of who she is.
	Ending: They all make a relaxed trip to the Golden Temple of Amritsar.
The author	Rachel Anderson lives in Norfolk with her family, one of whom required a chaperone for a visit to India, providing the subject of this book. Heinemann will send a reprint of pages from the author's notebook. Author of several novels for children, Rachel Anderson won the Guardian Children's Fiction Award for her novel *Paper Faces* in 1992. Her most recent book is *Letters from Heaven*.
Activities	• Section A's language activity aims to increase awareness of the Scottish dialect words in the book, through scanning the book, making an informed guess at meaning and then confirming through access to a dialect dictionary or a native speaker. • Section B will aid pupils in using the author's words to visualise setting. • Section C enables pupils to appreciate that the novel, whilst in the third person, focuses largely on Jazz's view of things. Yet all the people she comes into contact with must have reactions to her; some may be sympathetic and understanding of her difficult life; some may just find her rude and aggressive. The activities give practice in writing in different genres and from different viewpoints.
Assessment	The ability to: • scan text and use a two-way checking process (context and dictionary/human resource) to arrive at the meaning of dialect words; • visualise setting using author's description; • perceive and express points of view not explicitly stated in the text.
Related reading	*The Secret Garden* by Frances Hodgson Burnett; *Comfort Herself* by Geraldine Kaye; *Thunder and Lightnings* by Jan Mark; *The Way to Sattin Shore* by Philippa Pearce

# 15 Princess Jazz and the Angels

by Rachel Anderson

Page references are to the Mammoth 1995 paperback edition.

A *While reading the book or after reading the book*

1 Write down the meaning of the following Scottish dialect words, making sure that they fit the context. Then check how near you were by using a dialect dictionary or asking a native speaker.

clarty	culchie	greetin	peelie-wally
besom	bide	teenie	flit
footer	wheesh	gallus	stushie
wean	tumshie	rammy	deaving
fykie	cuddy	feart	skellie
couthie	carline	fou	wheesht
feartie	puggie	tranchled	…

B 2 The main places in which the action takes place in this book are: Jazz and her mother's flat in Glasgow, the foster parents' home, the airports and the aeroplane, the home of Jazz's relations in the Punjab, the hospital and the Golden Temple of Amritsar. Imagine you are making a film of this book. Using the author's descriptions, draw plans with some helpful notes for one or more of these locations.

C *All these activities should include a discussion with your partner, group or teacher.*

3 *Read or re-read up to page 28.* Write the report that Miss MacFadyen, the social worker, will have to write about Jazz.

4 Write a scene from a play where the foster parents have just said good-bye to Jazz as she leaves for the airport and are discussing the experience of having had her to stay.

5 *Read or re-read up to page 47.* Jazz writes a letter to her mother which is pure fantasy. Assuming one of the relations can write in fluent English, write to Bridie from one of them, expressing reactions to Jazz's arrival and her first few days with them.

6 *Read or re-read up to page 62.* Jazz and her grandmother (Oldest Auntiji) really don't understand one another and the story comes to a crisis when Jazz offends her and then runs away. Write the prayer that Oldest Auntiji might have uttered after this incident.

7 *Read or re-read to the end of the book.* Through the care of her relations and of Dr Elspeth, Jazz begins to believe that there *are* 'angels' who look after her and she begins to feel surer of herself and not so angry. Imagine that Dr Elspeth helps her to make ten resolutions which she'll try to keep. Write those resolutions.

CRACKING GOOD BOOKS © Judith Graham 1997

16 The Pied Piper of Hamelin

by Robert Browning
Illustrated by André Amstutz
First published by Orchard Books, 1993; in paperback by Orchard Books, 1994
ISBN 1 85213 651 0
This version slightly abridged

Genre	Rhyming, narrative poem, picture book
Narrative voice	Third person, informal narrator
Theme	Greed and the price to be paid if promises are broken
Characters	The people and children of Hamelin, the Mayor and the town councillors, the Pied Piper, the lame boy, rats
Setting	The town and surroundings of Hamelin, Germany
Era	Around 1300 AD. (Many children had disappeared from Hamelin at the time of the Crusades.)
Language	Figurative: Simile: eyes 'like a candle flame where salt is sprinkled', the council stood 'as if they were changed into blocks of wood', 'sparrows were brighter than peacocks'; metaphor: 'the mayor quaked', 'magic slept in his quiet pipe'
	Use of standard/dialect: Standard throughout
	Use of direct speech: Some, but majority is narration
	Other: Archaic: 'when begins my ditty', 'quoth', 'ere', 'a wondrous portal'; formal: 'quaint attire', 'a lost endeavour'; word order: 'when begins my ditty', 'his steps addressed', 'nor suffered they'
Story structure	Opening: Hamelin, though a most pleasant town, is plagued with rats. The people angrily demand of their Mayor and his councillors that something be done.
	Inciting moment: At their wits' end, the councillors appear to be saved by the arrival of a quaint figure, the Pied Piper, who, for a sum of 1,000 guilders, promises to rid the town of the rats.
	Development: So relieved are the Mayor and his team that they offer 50,000 but in the event, once the rats are drowned in the river, they break their word to the Pied Piper and offer a mere 50 guilders.
	Denouement: The Pied Piper is not to be trifled with and, just as he bewitched the rats by the sweetness of his piping, so he draws all Hamelin's children behind him and leads them from the town, never to return. Only a lame child remains.
	Ending: The town of Hamelin commemorates its lost children to this day.
The author	Robert Browning (1812–1889) published this poem in 1842. Amongst his other poems, perhaps the best known are *Porphyria's Lover*, *My Last Duchess* and *How They Brought the Good News from Ghent to Aix*.
The illustrator	André Amstutz is best known as the witty illustrator of some of Allan Ahlberg's books, including the *Funnybones* series, *Happy Families* and *Ten in a Bed*.
Activities	• Section A encourages empathy with the main character; • Section B consolidates understanding and predictive abilities; • Section C aids recall and understanding of the main event of the story; • Section D encourages presentation of the poem's content in a different form.
Assessment	The ability to: • discuss feelings, empathise, recall events and represent in a suitable form; • take on several different genres.
Related reading	Other rhyming classic narrative poems are *The Highwayman* by Alfred Noyes (see page 58); *Matilda*, by Hilaire Belloc; *The Rime of the Ancient Mariner* by S.T. Coleridge and *The Lady of Shalott* by Alfred Lord Tennyson.

16 The Pied Piper of Hamelin

by **Robert Browning**

Illustrated by André Amstutz

A *Before reading the book*

1 Spend 5–10 minutes in your group discussing a time when someone promised something and then the promise was broken. You need to think about: why the promise was made, why the promise was broken, how you felt, whether you felt like taking revenge, whether you did take revenge.

B *Half-way through the book*

2 Look back at the first full opening at the start of the poem. Put yourself in the shoes of either the woman raking in the field or one of the fishermen. You should then write a diary entry for your character. You should stress how pleasant it is to live in Hamelin but how the rats are becoming unbearable. Invent particular atrocities that the rats have been responsible for. Stop your entry before the Pied Piper comes to town.

3 Read up to the point where the Pied Piper is offered only 50 guilders; share your predictions of how the story will continue. Jot down your ideas so you can look back when you have read the whole poem.

C *After reading the book*

4 At the end of the poem, the Mayor forbids any music or dancing or drinking in the street where the children left the town.

Either:

Create a warning poster, using appropriate language and illustration.

Or:

Write the 'story on a column' which tells the world how the children were stolen away.

D 5 Make a list of the typical attractions that you might find in a tourist pamphlet, for example museums, wall plaques, statues, churches, processions, performances, souvenir shops, guided walks. Now create a tourist pamphlet for Hamelin which particularly focuses on the legend of the Pied Piper. The poem tells us there is a stained glass window; it could be described. In addition, you may like to know that, in modern Hamelin, a clockwork piper moves, twice a day, round the clock tower of the town hall, followed by clockwork rats and children. There is also a street known as Bungenlosenstrasse, the street without a drum, and a plaque in the wall of the 'Rat-Catcher's House' which tells the world how the children were stolen away.

CRACKING GOOD BOOKS © Judith Graham 1997

17 The Wreck of the Zanzibar

by Michael Morpurgo
Illustrated by Christian Birmingham
First published by Heinemann, 1995; in paperback by Mammoth, 1995
ISBN 0 7497 2620 2
Winner of the Whitbread Children's Book Award, 1995

Genre	Historical, realistic novel
Narrative voice	The main story (in letter and diary format) is framed by a first person narration.
Theme	Rural survival in the early 20th century, family relationships, faith
Characters	Laura, 14, her twin brother Billy, their parents and Grandmother May. Michael, the adult recipient of the diary in the modern era, is Laura's great nephew.
Setting	Bryher, one of the Scilly Isles, off the coast of Cornwall; harsh weather
Era	Initially, and finally, modern day. The diary is of ten months in 1907.

Language

Figurative: Simple similes and metaphors: the house creaks in the wind 'like a ship at sea', 'great green wall of water'; some alliteration: 'shredded sails'; personification: the gig 'groaned and cried', hope is 'harder to mend than roofs'

Use of standard/dialect: Standard English throughout

Use of direct speech: Laura's diary includes a small amount of direct speech.

Other: Some technical terms related to the sea and rural life

Story structure

Opening (framing narrative): The narrator, Michael, travels to Brhyer to the funeral of his great aunt Laura. At the reading of the will, he is given a package with a personal letter from Laura and her girlhood diary.

Opening (diary narrative): The diary starts on January 20th 1907, the day that Laura is fourteen. She writes of family life, the hardships that have to be borne and particularly of Billy, her twin, who does not get on well with their father. Laura is angry that her father prevents her rowing in the gig.

Inciting moment: Lured by a passing sailor's tales, Billy runs away to sea. Gloom descends. Mother becomes withdrawn, ferocious storms result in the destruction of homes and livelihoods. The future looks bleak.

Development: Laura finds a leatherback turtle stranded on the beach. She knows that it should be used for food but she and her grandmother, secretly, return it to the sea. The situation worsens and the family is thinking of leaving the island. A ship is wrecked during a further storm. Laura replaces her injured father in the rescue gig and finds her brother amongst the wrecked sailors.

Denouement: The ship, named the *Zanzibar*, is full of cargo, including cows, and the fortunes of the islanders are reversed.

Ending: One last item is washed up: the boat's figurehead, a wooden turtle.

Ending (framing narrative): Michael, and his nephews and nieces, place the turtle (as Laura has willed) on the village green for all to play on.

The author — Michael Morpurgo, originally a teacher and storyteller, is now the author of over fifty books, including several award-winners.

The illustrator — The soft pencil drawings which Christian Birmingham made for this book are characteristic of his work, though he has recently illustrated *Oliver Twist* in full colour.

Activities

The activities aim to:
- draw out key moments in the plot;
- contrast the characters of brother and sister;
- reflect upon setting and detail;
- invent appropriate dialogue.

Assessment

The ability to:
- assess character;
- develop critical ability;
- follow plot and isolate key moments;
- write direct speech to suit situation and character.

Related reading — *Grace* by Jill Paton Walsh, *So Far from Skye* by Judith O'Neill and *The Butterfly Lion* by Michael Morpurgo

17 The Wreck of the Zanzibar

by **Michael Morpurgo**
Illustrated by Christian Birmingham

Page references are to the Mammoth 1995 paperback edition.

Before you start reading the book use a map of the British Isles to find where the Scilly Isles are. (The hardback version of the book includes maps on its end papers.)

A 1 Imagine that Billy and his sister are able to exchange letters with each other whilst Billy is away at sea and Laura's life on the island is becoming more and more harsh. Write a pair of letters, using the information of the book closely. Try to bring out the different characters of the twins and show how each feels about their father and their mother and their current life.

B 2 One of the things that Laura wants more than anything else is to row in the gig. At the end, she does eventually get to do this (pages 90–102) but only because her father is injured, not because he sees she is ready for it. Because her brother turns up almost immediately, Laura's moment is overshadowed. Some readers are disappointed by this part of the book. Discuss these points in your group and rewrite the ending, taking account of the group's ideas for what would make a satisfactory conclusion.

C 3 Did the illustrations in the book add to your appreciation of the book? You might like to consider them under the following headings: the clothes, homes and boats of the time; the loneliness of the island; the rural nature of the life; the sea.

Either: choose one illustration that you particularly liked and describe it.

Or: decide on one more full page illustration that you would like to have had and describe it, showing how it would add to the book.

D 4 The main part of the book is the story told by Laura in her 1907 diary. Generally, writers of diaries do not include the actual speech of other people – they usually just summarise speech or report it indirectly. In order to keep the diary lively, Michael Morpurgo, the author, does give his readers some direct speech but much less than a third person narrative might usually have. Your task is to choose a key scene and rewrite it, supplying all the speech as you think it might have actually been. It doesn't matter if the scene has a little direct speech already: develop and extend the scene, keeping close to the detail the writer has supplied.

Note

You might be interested to know that Michael Morpurgo *did* find a wrecked ship's figurehead – of a dolphin, not a turtle – and that he *does* go to the Scilly Isles but that the fiction of 'Michael' receiving a letter and a diary from an aunt is just that: a fiction. The basis of a subsequent Morpurgo novel, with a 'Michael' character, *The Butterfly Lion*, is rooted in fact however.

18
Five Children and It

by E. Nesbit
Illustrated by
H.R. Millar
First published by
T. Fisher Unwin,
1902; in
paperback by
Puffin Books,
1959
ISBN
0-14-035061-6

Genre	Adventure/magic
Narrative voice	Third person, with regular direct authorial comments
Theme	Holiday family life, wasted wishes
Characters	The children: Cyril (Squirrel), Anthea (Panther), Jane (Pussy), Robert (Bobs) and the baby (Lamb); their mother; Martha, their servant; numerous smaller parts, for example a vicar and his wife and servant, shopkeepers, gypsies (sic), Red Indians (sic), circus owners; It – the Psammead (pronounced Sammyadd)
Setting	Rural Edwardian England
Era	Turn of the century
Language	**Figurative:** Not a great deal. The Psammead is described using similes. Occasional alliterative build-up of adjectives: 'thorny, thistly, briery, brambly'; some metaphor: 'the sea changed its lodgings'; some puns: 'before you take other people's tongues'
	Use of standard/dialect: Some dialect in the dialogue of characters: 'How this bolt do stick!' Some satirical imitation of the literary speech of historical romances: 'Grammercy for thy courtesy, fair sir knight.'
	Direct speech: a fair amount – more than is common in a book of this period.
	Other: Surprisingly accessible language; some expressions now regarded as affected: 'brekker', 'rather decent', 'I say', 'do dry up a sec'; archaisms: 'we're no forrader' and terms which are no longer in use: 'fly' (carriage); 'Norfolks' (belted jackets); over-scrupulous grammar: 'Everyone got its legs kicked'; grandiosity: 'chivalry was a stranger to the breast of the baker's boy'; rhetorical flourishes: repeating phrases, such as 'the necessities of life'.
Story structure	**Opening:** The family arrives for a holiday in rural England. Mother and father immediately called away.
	Inciting moment: In the gravel pit at the side of the house, the children dig in the sand and unearth an ancient, magic sand fairy, the Psammead.
	Development: The Psammead grants the children one wish a day lasting until sunset. Through immaturity, accident, foolishness and other reasons, the children's wishes never yield the expected results, often bringing great anxiety and embarrassment, not only to themselves.
	Denouement: The Psammead uses its last wish to extricate the children and their mother from a difficult situation.
	Ending: The author hints that any further encounters with the Psammead belong to another book.
The author	E. Nesbit, 1858–1924, was known for her lively family/fantasy stories for children. She had several children of her own.
The illustrator	H. R. Millar lived from 1869 until 1940 and contributed line drawings to many children's novels.
Activities	• Section A enables identification of the patterned structure of wish and result; • Section B develops a socio-critical response to the book.
Assessment	The ability to: • perceive and replicate the narrative pattern in the book; • make an evaluative response.
Related reading	Many of Nesbit's novels, for example *The Railway Children*, are still in print. Other books of the period are *The Little Princess* and *The Secret Garden* by Frances Hodgson Burnett.

CRACKING GOOD BOOKS

18 Five Children and It

by E. Nesbit
Illustrated by H.R. Millar

A *While reading the book*

1 In the chart below you will see a list of the children's wishes which the Psammead grants. Copy it out and, against each wish, write the result, trying if you can to quote directly from the book. The first one is done for you.

Then, add one further wish of your own invention and write the result. If you wish, develop this idea into a whole new chapter.

Wish	Result
1 *To be as beautiful as the day*	The children become 'radiantly beautiful' and only just identify each other. The Lamb doesn't recognise them, nor does Martha and so they are kept out of the house and very hungry until they return to their own 'nice and ugly' selves.
2 *To be rich beyond dreams*	
3 *To have the Lamb wanted by everybody*	
4 *To have wings to fly with*	
5 *To be in a besieged castle*	
6 *To be bigger than the baker's boy*	
7 *To have the Lamb grown up*	
8 *To have Red Indians in England*	
9 *To have Lady Chittenden's jewels at home*	
10	

B

2 *Five Children and It* was written in 1902 and the author was brought up with servants, a situation which she probably never questioned. She also probably never questioned commonly-held views about gypsies (Travellers), American Indians, making money out of exploiting Africa, and the mentally ill, all of which she views in ways unacceptable to us now. Does this mean that we should not read books written so long ago? What are your views? Try to give examples from the book to support your argument. It may be that you would like to write a letter which outlines your views to the publisher.

3 The author of this book is very keen to show how honesty and proper behaviour must be encouraged in young people. The children are worried if they have not paid properly for something or feel that they have let somebody down. In this way, the author attempts to pass on to her child readers a strong sense of right and wrong. Can you find examples of these moments in the book? Do you think authors should teach children about morals? Which modern authors do this? Prepare a talk on this to the rest of your group or class.

19 The Stinky Cheese Man and Other Fairly Stupid Tales

by Jon Scieszka
Illustrated by Lane Smith
First published by Viking, USA, 1992; in paperback by Puffin Books, 1993
ISBN 0-14-054896-3

Genre	Humorous, subversive, post-modern picture book or, as the book's publication data says, 'madcap revisions of traditional fairy tales'
Narrative voice	Jack, the narrator and compiler of the book, speaks directly to the reader and interacts with the characters within the stories which he tells. The physical features of the book are also part of the story, for example the Little Red Hen complains about the ISBN guy.
Theme	Exploding literary and book-making conventions
Characters	Jack, the narrator and compiler of the book; various fairy tale characters, including the Little Red Hen and the Giant
Setting	A topsy-turvy, fairy tale world
Era	Timeless
Language	Figurative: Very little
	Use of standard/dialect: Standard throughout
	Use of direct speech: Direct speech in the stories and also when the reader is addressed directly by Jack, for example 'Turn the page over quietly.'
	Other: Technical terms from book-making, for example cover, end papers, title page, dedication page, introduction, table of contents, narrator, author, illustrator, font size, upper and lower case letters. Some Americanisms and colloquialisms, for example 'Every time he met a nice girl, his mom and dad would pile one hundred mattresses on top of a pea and then invite her to sleep over.'
Story structure	Opening: Jack interrupts the Little Red Hen who is asking who will help her make her bread on the end papers even before the book has started.
	Development: Jack, after a title page labelled Title Page, a dedication page upside down and an introduction that dissuades its readers from reading it, starts telling various tales. The Table of Contents kills off Chicken Licken and three other stories get subverted before Jack meets the giant who makes him tell stories to save his life. Several other stories follow and the giant falls asleep. Jack takes his opportunity to move the end papers up to kid the giant that the book is over.
	Denouement: The Little Red Hen has finally made her bread and the giant wakes up on hearing words about food.
	Ending: Jack escapes but the Little Red Hen becomes the giant's sandwich.
The author and illustrator	Both men are American and have been awarded several prizes for their work.
Activities	• Section A aims to get pupils to read and retell some of the original fairy tales in the book. They are also helped to write a 'madcap' tale of their own. • Section B considers the role of the illustration and, using similar techniques, ask pupils to illustrate their own stories.
Assessment	The ability to: • scan a text; • research the original tales; • retell a story; • use the book's literary devices; • subvert a story themselves which they can illustrate.
Related reading	Jon Scieszka wrote *The Book that Jack Wrote* and *The Frog Prince Continued*. Lane Smith wrote and illustrated *Glasses, Who Needs 'Em?* and *The Big Pets*. Together they have created *The True Story of the Three Little Pigs* and *Maths Curse*. See also books by Janet and Allan Ahlberg, including *One Dark and Stormy Night*, and Quentin Blake and John Yeoman's *The Do-it-yourself House that Jack Built*.

19
The Stinky Cheese Man and Other Fairly Stupid Tales

by Jon Scieszka
Illustrated by
Lane Smith

A 1 a) In your pair, make a list of the titles of the traditional stories that are used in the book. You should be able to find about 12 titles altogether (excluding the one-liners in the giant's story).

b) Now take one of these traditional stories and tell it to your partner. You may need to read the original stories again first.

c) Now turn in the book to where the stories you have chosen have been reworked. Write two accounts, showing some of the changes. You don't need to re-tell the whole story. *The Princess and the Pea* has been done for you here as an example.

Original story
A princess is kept awake all night because she can feel the pea through the hundred mattresses and so the king and queen know she is a true princess and fit to marry their son. The prince doesn't do anything dishonest.

Reworked story
The prince is so keen on one girl that he makes sure she has a sleepless night by cheating. He puts a huge bowling ball under her mattresses. Not surprisingly, she feels it all night long. His parents don't find out and the prince and princess live happily ever after. Princes and princesses in fairy stories aren't usually allowed to be 'happy ever after' if they cheat.

2 You probably know other traditional stories which could be played around with and changed. Take one well-known story (not from this book) and change it in some way. Then write it up and keep it for using in Section B.

Here are some titles of stories to start you thinking. You may use another title but make sure it is well known.

Snow White and the Seven Dwarfs   Puss in Boots
Three Billy Goats Gruff   The Shoemaker and the Elves
The Great Big Enormous Turnip   The Three Little Pigs
Rapunzel   Hansel and Gretel

Remember how the makers of *The Stinky Cheese Man and Other Fairly Stupid Tales* changed the stories. They:

- mixed up one story with another one;
- had rather tragic instead of happy endings;
- made nothing much happen when you were expecting a lot;
- had the cheating people getting away with things;
- changed a character's name to something funny or revolting;
- introduced realism into the story and ended it rather abruptly.

B 3 The illustrator of *The Stinky Cheese Man and Other Fairly Stupid Tales* has made many of his pictures by using scraps of material, photographs, newsprint and other people's illustrations to create a collage effect. Design and then create a collage poster to advertise or illustrate the story you wrote in activity 2. You will need to collect together as many odd scraps of material as you can find. Share them around in your group. Look back at how Lane Smith has achieved his effects and compare his work with your group's efforts.

CRACKING GOOD BOOKS © *Judith Graham* 1997

20 The Firework-Maker's Daughter

by Philip Pullman

Illustrated by Nick Harris

First published by Doubleday, 1995; in paperback by Corgi Yearling, 1996
ISBN 0 440 86331 7
Winner of the Smarties Prize, 1996

Genre	Fantastical, action-packed, quest adventure
Narrative voice	Third person. Parallel narrative strands
Theme	The getting of wisdom
Characters	Lalchand, a firework-maker; his daughter, Lila, aged about 11; the King; the King's white elephant, Hamlet; Chulak, the elephant's servant; Rambashi, an entrepreneur; Goddess of the Emerald Lake; Razvani, the Fire-Fiend; three visiting firework-makers: Dr Puffenflasch, Signor Scorcini and Colonel Sam Sparkington
Setting	A 'country east of the jungle and south of the mountains', perhaps Indonesia. Rupees are the currency and sarongs are worn.
Era	A 'thousand miles (sic) ago' but with present day overtones
Language	**Figurative:** Some similes, alliteration: fingernails 'flickering like fireflies' **Use of standard/dialect:** Standard throughout **Use of direct speech:** Lively dialogue captures the different characteristics of the varied cast. **Other:** Inventive names for fireworks and their ingredients (see B2)
Story structure	**Opening:** The child Lila is growing up to be a talented firework-maker. **Inciting moment:** Lila discovers that her father is witholding essential firework-making secrets. Her friend Chulak extracts a part but only a part of the secret. Lila sets off to find Royal Sulphur from Razvani the Fire Fiend. **Development:** The distraught father berates Chulak and reveals that Lila must go armed with water, obtainable from the Goddess of the Emerald Lake. From this point several stories develop concurrently. Lila outmanoeuvres the comical Rambashi and his river pirates and makes a perilous journey to the Fire Fiend's Grotto. The white elephant and Chulak give the guards the slip, obtain the magic water and arrive at the fiery grotto with the precious protection just in time. Lalchand, implicated in the escape of the elephant, is thrown into prison. Rambashi turns up as an eccentric restaurateur. Lila comes through her fiery ordeal only to learn of her father's imprisonment. Execution is stayed only if Lila and her father can together win a firework display competition. **Denouement:** Amidst stiff competition, they succeed spectacularly and the celebrations include the re-emergence of Rambashi with a band of musicians. **Ending:** Lalchand explains to Lila that Royal Sulphur is a metaphor for wisdom, gained through suffering and risk. As she has the Three Gifts (talent, courage and luck) she can now be admitted into the firework-makers' secrets.
The author	Philip Pullman is the highly-acclaimed author of *Northern Lights*. He has also written the graphic novels *Spring-Heeled Jack* and *Count Karlstein*.
The illustrator	Born in 1958, Nick Harris trained at Harrow and has illustrated *King Arthur*, *Robin Hood* and *Wind in the Willows*. His most recent book is *Dragon Quest*.
Activities	The activities aim to: • examine the author's style, especially of descriptive passages; • examine and use the structure of the author's invented names; • reflect on and select qualities of the book.
Assessment	The ability to: • reflect on stylistic features and to recreate description; • analyse and recreate language and specific genre; • make a personal response in a review of the book.
Related reading	*Beaver Towers* by N. Hinton; *The Ice Palace* by R. Swindells

20
The Firework-Maker's Daughter

by Philip Pullman

Illustrated by Nick Harris

Page references are to the Corgi Yearling 1996 edition.

A 1 Philip Pullman has set his book in an imaginary country and describes his characters in a great range of extraordinary places. Look back at the part where Lila climbs up Mount Merapi (pages 51–54) and at the part where she is in Razvani's Grotto (pages 55–63). Prepare a reading of these sections and share them with your group. You should then be able to discuss how the author tells you what the mountain and the Grotto are like and also how Lila felt. It is clear that throughout this book the author does not only describe places; he always has people in the places who react and feel.

After your reading and discussion, see if you can write an extra scene, set somewhere extraordinary, with Lila (or Chulak and Hamlet) experiencing the place. Alternatively, you could write a scene set in the prison into which Lalchand has been thrown, keeping the description as close to Philip Pulman's own style as you can.

B 2 Philip Pullman invents some wonderful names for the fireworks in the story. Look carefully at the list below and then add more of your own invention. Notice how the first word describes noise, movement, colour, appearance or a place. It acts as an adjective. The second word is a noun, often a plural noun, and names an object or objects. If you follow this pattern you will find you can invent equally good names.

Fireworks

Crackle Dragons	Leaping Monkeys	Golden Sneezes
Java Lights	Tumbling Demons	Shimmering Coins
Krakatoa Fountain	Golden Serpents	Foaming Moss

Now add to the firework ingredients list. Notice that the words before the nouns in this list are more often other nouns or verbs, but that they still work as adjectives.

Ingredients

fly-away powder	thunder-grains	scorpion oil
spark repellent	glimmer juice	salts-of-shadow
powders of salt	doubling-back powder	fire-crystals
cloud-powder		

Now write a little book of instructions on how to make your firework and what ingredients are needed. Set it all out like a food recipe and add illustrations if you wish.

C This book won a major children's book award and many children wrote reviews of it which influenced the final decision. Write a review yourself, saying what *you* most enjoyed in the book.

21 Harvey Angell

by Diana Hendry
First published by Julia MacRae, 1991; in paperback by Random House, 1993
ISBN 0 09 995580 6
Winner of the Whitbread Prize, 1991

Genre	Mystery thriller, ghost story, fantasy, parable
Narrative voice	Third person, focus on Henry
Theme	The (re) discovery of 'energy' (i.e. warmth, love, delight) in life
Characters	Henry, an orphan living with his pinched, tea-bag counting Aunt Agatha in her boarding house which houses: the baker, Mr Murgatroyd, until he is replaced by the enigmatic Harvey Angell, Miss Muggins, Miss Skivvy and the aspiring poet, Mr Perkins
Setting	No. 131 Ballantyre Road, a tall, narrow boarding house 'with a roof that frowned over the top windows'. Churchyard and café
Era	Present day, with a sense of the past permeating
Language	**Figurative:** Abundant, witty and fluent use of simile, metaphor, idiom, alliteration, personification, puns, hyperbole. In particular, there is the extended metaphor of the 'connecting current' running through the book. **Use of standard/dialect:** Some non-standard English in the waitress' speech **Use of direct speech:** Abundant **Other:** A recurring rhyme: 'watts and volts, watts and volts, better by far than thunderbolts'; poems quoted; capitalisation used for dramatic/ironic effect: 'Aunt Agatha likes nothing better than a Big Saving and dislikes lodgers who have An Appetite.'
Story structure	**Opening and inciting moment:** Henry returns from school to find that his aunt has ejected the baker and is interviewing a replacement lodger for the tiny attic room. **Development:** Against all expectations, Aunt Agatha lets the room to Harvey Angell, 'a kind of electrician', whose apparent abstemiousness endears him to her. The household lightens up noticeably though there is a remaining sorrow and sharpness in Aunt Agatha, and Henry, though captivated, is curious. Henry (and Mr Perkins) follow Harvey Angell as he makes his way at dawn to the churchyard and there they realise that he has magical qualities. These are confirmed when Henry eavesdrops on Harvey Angell in the Waifs and Strays Café. Harvey's mission is to turn 131 Ballantyre Road from a house into a home. **Denouement:** Henry plays his part in diagnosing Aunt Agatha's sorrow. **Ending:** Connections made, Harvey Angell slips away leaving a legacy of happiness behind him. Henry takes over the attic.
The author	Diana Hendry, originally a journalist, is now a poet and teacher. She has written several children's books, including a sequel to *Harvey Angell*, to be published in 1997. *Harvey Angell* may become a film.
Activities	• Section A will help pupils gain an understanding of the figurative use of language which is so much a part of the enjoyment of the book; • Section B will help pupils review the book and to recognise the changes that Harvey Angell has effected.
Assessment	The ability to: • skim and scan and isolate particular literary/linguistic devices; • summarise and present key ideas succinctly in keeping with two of the genres (references and notes in a notebook) used in the novel.
Related reading	*Dear Mr Henshaw* by Beverley Cleary, *The Ghost Downstairs* by Leon Garfield, *The Phantom Tollbooth* by Norton Juster

21
Harvey Angell

by Diana Hendry

Page references are to the Random House 1993 paperback edition.

A 1 A large part of the humour in Harvey Angell lies in the way the author, Diana Hendry, uses language. She uses figurative language which goes beyond the straightforward and simple. An example is: 'Henry thinks that the lights up the side of the office blocks at night look like zips.' The author could have just described the lights as a pattern; something extra is added with the image of the zip.

The following list gives examples of the figurative language used in the book. Find other examples that you particularly like and add them under each heading.

Simile:
'Aunt Agatha, gaunt and stark as a winter tree' (page 16)

Metaphor:
'postage stamp of a room' (page 12)

Alliteration:
'stingy, scrimping Scrooge' (page 12) (Scrooge was a very mean accountant in Charles Dickens' novel *A Christmas Carol*)

Personification:
'the window panes rattled with alarm. Aunt Agatha gave them a look and they stopped.' (page 32)

Idiom:
'Fine words butter no parsnips.' (page 50)

The main game that the author plays with language is to use electrical terms to describe what has to be done to bring happiness back to the household. You should be able to collect up several of these metaphors.

B 2 On pages 41 and 42, you can read two short references given by people whom Harvey Angell has helped to become 'connected'. A reference recommends the work of an employee who is moving on. Imagine that Harvey returns to ask Aunt Agatha for a reference. Write the glowing(!) reference, if possible keeping the secret of his real work by using the electrical terms ambiguously.

3 We have read some of Henry's notes in his notebook (pages 75–76, 112–113). Write another entry (using invented spelling if you wish) which Henry might have written after Harvey has gone. There should be great changes and improvements to report on in the household.

CRACKING GOOD BOOKS © *Judith Graham* 1997

22 Children of Winter

by Berlie Doherty
Illustrated by Ian Newsham
First published by Methuen, 1985; in paperback by HarperCollins, Lions, 1986
ISBN 0-00-672583-X
and by Mammoth, 1996
ISBN 0-7497-1845-5
Televised by Channel 4

Genre	Time-slip historical
Narrative voices and devices	Third person, focusing on Catherine, a story within a story as present dissolves into the past
Theme	Resilience, survival without parents
Characters	The modern era family: Catherine, Patsy and Andrew Tebbutt (aged approximately 13, 10 and 6) and their parents; the 17th century Tebbutt family: Catherine (aged 13), Tessa (about 10) and Dan (aged 6), their mother; Maggie Hoggs, a woman crazed with grief; Dick Mossop, a villager; Clem, the shepherd
Setting	A cruck barn on the Derbyshire moors, during the winter
Era	Present day, slipping into 1666
Language	Figurative: Several similes: 'we were as foolish as hens'; occasional striking images: 'the sky was rushing into blackness' Use of standard/dialect: Derbyshire dialect in the dialogue of the 17th century characters: 'What a pair of tortoises tha'rt', 'Call thysen a Christian?' Other: Some striking terms: 'trickle-stream', 'thinking-log', 'shiver-shoes'
Story structure	Opening: The modern-day Tebbutt family leaves Sheffield by bus to visit their grandmother in the country. They cross over the moors on foot. They are drenched by rain and the father becomes separated from the rest of the family. Inciting moment: Catherine, strangely prescient, leads the others to an old cruck barn. Mother sets off to search for their father and the children play a game of pretending which slips into the past at the time of the plague. Development: The 17th century Tebbutt children have been taken to the cruck barn to avoid the plague which is ravaging their village. Their lives are filled with the practical tasks of feeding themselves, of getting warm, of keeping occupied and happy. Their mother can only have contact at a distance with them. Other encounters are both alarming (Maggie Hoggs) and productive (Dick Glossop) but eventually Clem the shepherd arrives and he brings the plague. Dan takes pity on him and, against orders, comforts him. Denouement: Dan develops symptoms of the plague. A knocking on the barn door brings the messenger who announces that the plague is over. Ending: The present-day children's father calls out that the storm is over and they all, with Andrew/Dan sneezing a little, resume their journey to their grandmother's house in the village below.
The author	Berlie Doherty was born in Liverpool and now lives outside Sheffield. She has been a teacher but has been writing professionally since 1980. Her work is often influenced by the moors around her and her contacts with children.
The illustrator	Ian Newsham is a freelance illustrator.
Activities	• Section A encourages reflection on the author's narrative skill in managing the time-shift, and helps children to envisage an unnarrated event and to predict the development of the story; • Section B supports children in their writing of an informed review.
Assessment	The ability to: • review author techniques and to make deductions and predictions; • write a reasoned review, backed by examples chosen from the book.
Related reading	Berlie Doherty's *Street Child* is another historical novel, this time set in the 19th century. *A Parcel of Patterns* by Jill Paton Walsh is also about the plague.

22 Children of Winter

by Berlie Doherty

A *After reading the first three chapters*

1. If you re-read the first chapter, you will understand many of Catherine's actions and comments to her family which they find strange and rather spooky, such as her plea to her mother that her father shouldn't go to their gran's. Can you scan the first chapter and find three more of these moments? Try to explain their significance.

2. In between chapters 2 and 3, something has happened 'off-stage' that means Catherine, Tessa and Dan will not be joined by their parents at the barn. We don't read about the parents' decision not to join their children but they must have made it at dawn when the mother visited the grandmother and discovered that she had the plague. (The father had stayed there overnight.) Re-read chapter 3. In pairs, act out or write the conversation that the parents must have had at the sick grandmother's bedside before they came to their sad decision.

3. Before you continue reading, share with others your thoughts about what will happen to the children on their own in the barn up on the moors. Write down two or three ideas so that when you have finished the book you can look back and see if your ideas and what actually happens have anything in common.

B *After reading the book*

4. The reasons that readers give for liking *Children of Winter* usually fall into one of these three categories:

   - They like the way the book slips into the past from the present day and back again at the end. They like checking that the author made the 'time-slipping' work properly, for example that she accounts at the very end for the absence of the cow and the hens.

   - They like the way the book creates a feeling of the children's lives in the 17th century and the struggle they had to remain alive and happy during the time of the plague. They like the historical details, such as the eating of the new vegetable potatoes and the need to keep a candle burning at all times.

   - They like the way lots of things happen in the story, especially when they thought at first that the children would just be isolated and that they would never meet anybody. They like the river scene with poor Maggie Hoggs and they find Dan's caring for Clem very touching.

   Why do you like the book? It may be that your reactions fall into one of the above categories or into more than one of them, or maybe you have different reasons of your own. Write a review of the book explaining why you like it and make sure that you give examples (as shown above) to show what you mean.

23 The Great Elephant Chase

by Gillian Cross
First published by Oxford University Press, 1992; in paperback by Puffin Books, 1994
ISBN 0-14-036361-0
Winner of the Smarties Prize, 1992, and the Whitbread Award, 1992

Genre	Journey adventure
Narrative voices	Third person narrative, with first person letters written by Cissie
Themes	Personal growth, friendship, animal care, good versus evil, survival
Characters	15 year old Tad; Cissie, an orphan after her father, Michael Keenan and sister Olivia are killed; Mr Jackson and Esther; Mr Nagel; the Stranger community; Miss Whitwell and others who help on the journey; Ketty and husband at the journey's end; Khush the elephant
Setting	Markle, an old mining town near Pittsburg, Pennsylvania, and the train, river and towns between it and Albery, Nebraska, USA
Era	The beginning of the 20th century
Language	**Figurative:** Language straightforward and concrete though occasional similes and metaphors stand out: the elephant's eye 'hidden in a cocoon of wrinkles', the boat devouring wood 'like a giant eating celery' **Use of standard/dialect:** Standard throughout with some attempt to catch the American speech patterns, the archaic language ('thee', 'thou') of the Stranger community, the German influenced speech of Mr Nagel **Use of direct speech:** Balance between direct speech and broadly narrative/descriptive passages **Other:** Letters, written by Cissie to Ketty, capture the rhythms, structures and vocabulary of written language a century ago
Story structure	**Opening:** The meek orphan Tad lives with and works for his Aunt Adah in Markle. In the same house live the unpleasant Mr Jackson and Esther. **Inciting moment:** Mr Keenan brings his amazing performing elephant and two daughters to town. Tad is accidentally locked into the elephant's wagon. **Development:** Tad is kept on in employment but a railway accident leaves Mr Keenan and Olivia dead. Mr Jackson turns up, claiming that he bought the elephant just before the crash. Cissie does not believe this and she, Tad and Khush travel down river on a raft, with Jackson and Esther in determined pursuit. Various heart-stopping adventures take place. **Denoument:** The party arrive exhausted at Ketty's in Nebraska. Jackson and Esther catch up and there is an unravelling of the ownership of the elephant. **Ending:** Tad, grown in assurance through his experiences, becomes the new owner of Khush.
The author	Gillian Cross has written around eighteen books, winning the Carnegie Medal for *Wolf* in 1991. *The Demon Headmaster* has been televised.
Activities	• Section A encourages the children to see how the book is plotted around a dramatic journey and chase, with events and character intertwining; • Section B is designed for children to see Tad's development. It also allows for different newsprint forms to be attempted.
Assessment	The ability to: • track events, map them to places, visualise the text; • assess character and development; • represent information.
Related reading	*Shaker Lane* by Alice and Martin Provensen, *Amish Adventure* by Barbara Smucker, *Bridge to Terebithia* by Katherine Paterson, *Little House in the Big Woods* series by Laura Ingalls Wilder

23
The Great Elephant Chase

by Gillian Cross

Page references are to the Puffin Books 1994 edition.

A *While reading the book*

1. It would be useful to have a large map of the USA. There is a very small map (which includes the author's imagined places) in the book. Using a roll of lining paper, transfer and enlarge the author's map on to as long a piece of lining paper as you can manage. Then, during your reading, plot the journeys of Tad, Khush, Cissie, and of Mr Jackson and Esther away from Markle and through their many adventures on their journey to Nebraska. It may be helpful to use different colour pens for the different characters. At or near certain key locations, for example Pittsburg, Eastcote's Landing, Cairo, St Louis, indicate important events and the arrival of new characters. You can illustrate your map.

2. If time allows, you could make a board game, perhaps rather like Snakes and Ladders, of *The Great Elephant Chase*, using as many of the events in the story as possible and bearing in mind the natures of the people involved. You may invent further incidents if you wish. Here are two suggestions to get you thinking: 'Khush has a split in his foot. Tad insists they rest for a day. Miss a turn.' and 'Cissie refuses to help clean out the flat boat. It takes Tad twice as long. Mr Jackson and Esther move forward three squares.'

B *This activity should be done after the book is completed, preferably with the whole class and after discussion and decision making.*

3. Tad moves off at the end of the book, with Khush now belonging to him and a character-forming experience behind him. But he will not go unnoticed of course with an elephant in tow. Imagine that the local *Nebraskan Times* does a special edition on Tad's story. Create this newspaper. It could include interviews back in Markle with Aunt Adah and with Mr Jackson and Esther but also with people who have a higher opinion of Tad, such as Mr Nagel if he is still alive (re-read pages 52–75), Mr Eastcote (re-read pages 103–125), Miss Whitwell (re-read pages 162–178), Cissie and Ketty and finally Tad himself. In addition, the newspaper could report on the rail crash in which Cissie's father and sister died, on the Stranger community and their beliefs, on elephants and where they come from and how they need to be looked after, on what the children ate on their journey, and so on. It could have a poster advertising Khush's next appearance or an article protesting at the use of live animals for entertainment. If the whole class has read the book, there can be many different items, based on the book, which can reflect particular interests and research.

24 The Finding

by Nina Bawden
First published by Victor Gollancz, 1985; in paperback by Puffin Books, 1987
ISBN 0-14-032698-7
Televised by Thames Television

Genre	Family story, mystery, intrigue
Narrative voice	Third person narrator
Theme	Family life, fairness, secrets and security
Characters	Alex (aged about 11); his adoptive family of mother and father, older sister Laura and two younger siblings, Bob and Ellie; Grandmother, her friend and neighbour Mrs Angel; Mrs Angel's nephew Mr Fowles; Grandmother's friend Major Bumpus; friends of the children, including Carla and Willy; the kindly but eccentric Poll and members of her alternative household: Sampson, Jake and Petal
Setting	London: Finsbury Fields, the embankment and the city
Era	Present day
Language	Figurative: Occasional vivid images: 'soapy dribble of spit'; mostly fairly straightforward and direct
	Use of standard/dialect: Standard throughout except in the Cockney dialect of the children who harass Alex, and of Poll and her 'family'
	Use of direct speech: Plentiful dialogue reveals the characters and their motives to the reader. Several characters defined by their idiomatic speech, for example the Major: 'Now. This feller, Fowles. Bit of a turn around, what?'
Story structure	Opening: The story starts dramatically with the circumstances of Alex's 'finding' as a baby in the arms of the Sphinx on the Embankment of the River Thames. We then jump to his eleventh 'founding' party with his family, within which certain tensions are evident, especially between mother and grandmother. Alex is taken by his grandmother to visit Mrs Angel who gives him a present of a photograph of her daughter, missing for twelve years.
	Development: Mrs Angel dies, her nephew behaves unpleasantly, particularly when it is learned that Mrs Angel has left everything to Alex. Alex's mother is keen to keep the legacy a secret but it leaks out in various ways and ultimately hits the headlines. Alex feels increasingly to blame for the family's altered circumstances and Laura can't avoid teasing him.
	Inciting moment: Alex runs away. He is eventually protected by Poll who takes him to join her unorthodox family of down-and-outs.
	Denouement: Amidst great family unhappiness and press attention, the Major focuses Laura's mind on where Alex might be and she eventually feels that she absolutely knows.
	Ending: Alex, released from Poll's home, is driven to central London and found by his family asleep in the arms of the Sphinx.
The author	Nina Bawden is a well-established, prize-winning author for children and adults. She writes perceptively of family emotions, motives, secrets and revelations.
Activities	• Section A sharpens perceptions of the main characters' impact on the story development. Pupils will need to use the text to support their statements. • Section B encourages pupils to think through some of the themes to their logical or possible conclusion.
Assessment	The ability to: • show understanding of some of the implied themes in the text and to respond to the complexity of the character delineation; • refer to the text when explaining views.
Related reading	*The Runaways* by Ruth Thomas, *The Secret Garden* by Frances Hodgson Burnett, *Goodnight Mr Tom* by Michelle Margorian

24 The Finding
by Nina Bawden

A *After reading the book*

1 Read the following statements and discuss them with a partner or in a group and then tick the box to show whether you agree, disagree or don't know.

a) Alex's grandmother likes to imagine that Alex's real mother is the long-lost daughter of her neighbour, Mrs Angel.
   Agree ☐   Disagree ☐   Don't Know ☐

b) Alex's grandmother is the cause of all the unhappiness.
   Agree ☐   Disagree ☐   Don't Know ☐

c) Alex's mother doesn't share enough information with her children.
   Agree ☐   Disagree ☐   Don't Know ☐

d) Alex's mother is really worried that someone will turn up and claim Alex and take him away.
   Agree ☐   Disagree ☐   Don't Know ☐

e) Alex's mother is the cause of all the unhappiness.
   Agree ☐   Disagree ☐   Don't Know ☐

f) Laura is jealous and spiteful towards Alex.
   Agree ☐   Disagree ☐   Don't Know ☐

g) Laura is the cause of all the unhappiness.
   Agree ☐   Disagree ☐   Don't Know ☐

h) Alex's grandmother, mother and sister all contribute to Alex's misery.
   Agree ☐   Disagree ☐   Don't Know ☐

i) Alex is a coward to run away. Running away doesn't solve anything.
   Agree ☐   Disagree ☐   Don't Know ☐

j) Both Alex and Laura compete for their parents' love.
   Agree ☐   Disagree ☐   Don't Know ☐

Give evidence taken from the book to support one of the statements with which you agree.

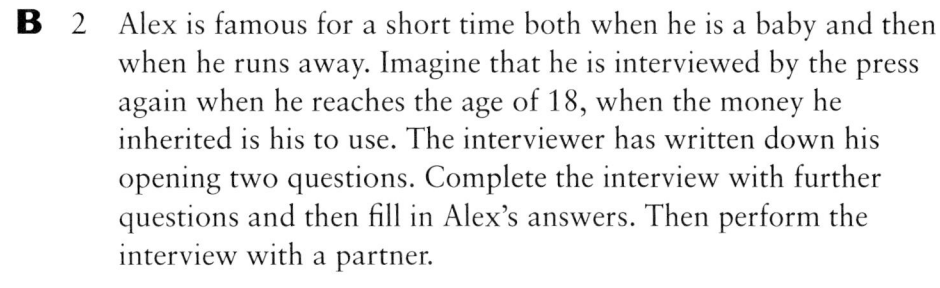

B 2 Alex is famous for a short time both when he is a baby and then when he runs away. Imagine that he is interviewed by the press again when he reaches the age of 18, when the money he inherited is his to use. The interviewer has written down his opening two questions. Complete the interview with further questions and then fill in Alex's answers. Then perform the interview with a partner.

> Can you remember what you felt when as an eleven year old you inherited all this money?
>
> Did you really understand what was happening when you ran away?

CRACKING GOOD BOOKS © Judith Graham 1997   79

Note

Judith Graham and NATE/YPS would be interested to receive any responses to *Cracking Good Books* from teachers who have undertaken any of the activities in their classrooms. We would welcome accounts of practice and examples of written work which could be used for a forthcoming book *Cracking Good Books in Practice*. We believe that there is a shortage of exemplar material in this area and that such a book would be useful and interesting to many teachers. Any work used would be fully acknowledged and each contributing teacher would receive a copy of the new book. We look forward to hearing from you.

NATE
50 Broadfield Road
Sheffield S8 0XJ